...quash, Maktumpus and Naunawauk...
...in Consideration of four Guns, foure Broad Cloth
...tts ten Shirts, ten paire of Stockings, forty pound
...of Beere to be payed as by their bill under
...e given granted Bargained and sold aliened conveyed ...
...ly give grant Bargain Sell Aliene Convey and Confirm
...all houses ...ent in Stratford in the Colloney...
...the Colloney of Connecticutt. Butted and Bounded
...and Land of Mr Sherman and on... Rogers...
...ds of Danbury North East on Land purchased
...on Land of Nummawaug an Indian the line
...tabuck. the sd Tract of Land Containing in length
...s with all Appurtenances privileges apur-
...pertaining to them the said William Janes
...s and Assignes to have and to hold for ever
...forever and we the sd Maunquash Massumpus
...d ministrators do Covenant promise and grant
...and Samuel Hawley their heirs and Assignes
...of the above Bargained prem...

Directions and Images

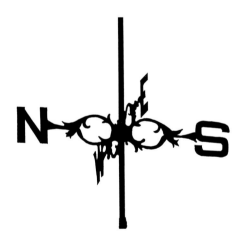

The League of Women Voters of Newtown, Inc.
1989

ISBN 0-9623444-0-0

Printed in the United States of America
Eastern Press, Inc.
New Haven, Connecticut

Typesetting, Computer Graphics and Layout
Barbara Dunn
Newtown, Connecticut

Cover Design: Greene, Dunn & Keith
Cover Photography: Joseph I. Kugielsky

CONNECTICUT

Directions and Images

Published by
The League of Women Voters of Newtown, Inc.
Ann Krane, President

Literary Director
Carole Telfair

Art Director
Carolyn Greene

Editors
Carole Telfair
Mary Jane (Bunny) Madden

Assistant Editors
Julie Stern
Judith Ince Craven

Writers
Carole Telfair
Julie Stern
Shirley Ferris
Bill Brassard
Nancy Doniger
Joanne Greco Rochman
Colleen Ferris Kimball
Mae S. Schmidle
Mary Mitchell
Scott Benjamin
Mark McGrath
Laura Lerman

Graphic Designers
Carolyn Greene
Barbara Dunn
Shari Keith

Business Editors
Patricia Denlinger
Judy S. Furlotte

Publicity
Elizabeth Wefer
Eleanor Zolov
Joan Fuest

Dedication

Since our community's earliest days, the networks of government, the common welfare, and the social fabric to hold townspeople together in work and play have been dependent on the most important of all of Newtown's historical figures — the volunteer.

This giant in our story has helped determine the directions and heightened the images of our town by service in many guises: as high office holder, fire fighter, planter of seeds, guide to youth, provider of services from lifelines to carpools. The contribution has been immense, the benefit beyond calculation.

Therefore, this book is dedicated to that all important force: to them, to you, to us all — the volunteers of Newtown, past, present, and future.

In Appreciation

We are indebted to many. Our first and best thanks go to the committee members with whom we spent numerous hours planning, working, and making decisions. In the art and design department, Shari Keith and Barbara Dunn, and in the editorial department, Bunny Madden — all have our gratitude, our respect, and our friendship.

The early editorial decisions were enhanced by the ideas and recommendations of Julie Stern and Judy Craven. Their contributions to the effort are greatly appreciated.

Caroline Stokes, with her immense knowledge of the Cyrenius H. Booth Library's historical collection, made suggestions that saved researchers literally hours of work in locating good stories and avenues of study. Her cooperation and the "open vault" policy at the library have been invaluable. We also wish to thank members of the library staff, especially Maureen Armstrong and Director Janet Woycik for their frequent and enthusiastic assistance.

Dan Cruson has been a very special resource. His consultation with several of our writers on several topics proved to be exceptionally helpful, as was his proofreading.

Specialized information on the Indians of this area was provided by Director of Education Trude Richmond of the American Indian Archaeological Institute in Washington, Connecticut.

Members of the staff of *The Newtown Bee* have been most gracious in answering questions and sharing photo files. We are also grateful to Frank Dunn for expert advice on the proper use of religious terms and titles throughout the book.

The writers, artists, and photographers who have devoted so much of their talents and time to this project have been mentioned in the text, but we wish to extend here a special acknowledgment of their contributions. Steven Kellogg has once again demonstrated his good will towards Newtown by donating drawings. Likewise, illustrator and town newcomer Ed Little has been most generous in helping to guarantee the high quality of art work in this volume.

Townspeople have perhaps run into professional photographers Joseph Kugielsky and Ken Kast in the act of capturing Newtown for posterity. We owe the character and excellence of photography to their high standards, and to those of fellow professionals Linda Napier and Mary Mitchell and to dedicated and skillful amateurs Dave Kriger, Pat McNally, Jim Gunn, and Jim Bird of the Flagpole Photographers.

Our writers have come from many and varied professional and amateur backgrounds. Their work has helped us achieve the rich texture that is evident in this book. Thanks to professionals Shirley Ferris, Bill Brassard, Mark McGrath, Scott Benjamin, and Joanne Rochman and to gifted writers Julie Stern, Nancy Doniger, Colleen Kimball, Mae Schmidle, Mary Mitchell, and Laura Lerman.

Proofreading is a trying but very necessary part of a project such as this. Our gratitude is due to Thomas Northcott, Ann Krane, and Judy Craven for their thorough job.

This book was published by the League of Women Voters of Newtown, Inc. We thank our fellow members of that organization for their backing, their encouragement, and their active participation in the process. Pat Denlinger and Judy Furlotte, along with President Ann Krane and members past and present, have dedicated themselves to the funding of this project. Special mention must go to Zee Northcott and to publicity committee members Elizabeth Wefer, Eleanor Zolov, and Joan Fuest.

Newtown, Past and Present has been presented in two previous editions. There was also an attempt to republish in 1983. Each of these projects involved the efforts of many League and community volunteers — to them we are grateful for the firm foundation of this work. Indexing efforts of the *Bee* and early planning and outlining by former resident Sue Polgar saved many of us hours of preliminary research. Two more ex-Newtowners, Joanna Martin and Betty Smith, contributed to the new sections on Newtown's pre-colonial inhabitants and the culture scene, respectively. We are grateful to them and hope that they will consider themselves very much a part of this project.

We have mentioned the community contribution to *Newtown, Connecticut: Directions and Images.* Our thanks go to all those citizens who communicated to us their suggestions and resources. We hope you'll enjoy this book and recognize the Newtown of your memories in it.

Lastly, we would like to thank Bill, Alexandra, and Julie Greene, and Bill, Megan, and Caty Telfair. Their comments and suggestions, their support, and especially their patience have been significant contributions to this project.

Carole Telfair
Carolyn Greene

Newtown, Connecticut
October, 1989

photograph courtesy of *The Newtown Bee*

Table of Contents

photograph by David Kriger

prologue

The Pre-Colonial Period

The Lay of the Land

Perhaps the most fitting way to begin a story of Newtown is to search out her most ancient history. It is evident all around us, a tale told by the last glacier, which did so much to sculpt this hilly area in the highlands of western Connecticut.

Following several previous glacial periods going back more than a million years, the last great ice sheet (which was at least several thousand feet thick) left town about 15,000 years ago. It was gradually retreating north after an initial advance to Long Island. The glacier rounded what had been jagged hills and deposited many rocks and boulders. Melting in place, its waters carried sediments downhill to create sand and gravel banks in some places. Very firm, clay-like (or hardpan) soils were left behind in other locations.

Geological evidence points to the existence of a large glacial pond or lake that covered a broad area roughly corresponding to today's Pootatuck River valley. Sand and gravel deposits were left along what much later became Route 25 in southern Newtown and down through the Pootatuck valley to Sandy Hook center. Under this same area lies the Pootatuck Aquifer, supply source for today's Newtown Water Company — another legacy of the glacier. Other sand and gravel deposits were left in Hawleyville and along Pogund Brook, Pond Brook, and the Aspetuck River.

The swamps of Newtown, such as the old Pine Swamp on Swamp Road, the Deep Brook Swamp off Route 302, and swamps on Key Rock Road and in Hawleyville, were a result of the poorly-draining hardpan that the glacier left behind.

Taunton Pond was formed by the glacier's retreat. Other bodies of water, however, such as Lakes Zoar and Lillinonah, Morgan's Pond in Hattertown, and Warner Pond in the Berkshire district of Sandy Hook were formed by human inhabitants eons later.

Drumlins, sloped and elliptical glacial hills that are oriented in the same direction as the glacier's advance, are also a feature of Newtown. Characterized by the hardpan soil, drumlins are to be found especially in the Taunton area.

In size, Newtown's 60.38 square miles make it the fifth largest town in Connecticut. The landscape is marked by rolling hills with a half dozen or so places reaching elevations of between 600 and 800 feet. The highest points in town are Taunton Hill (830 feet above sea level) and Castle Hill (690 feet).

The Housatonic River serves as the northeastern boundary, separating Newtown from Southbury. A second natural boundary is to the southeast, where the Halfway River and its confluence with the Housatonic mark the line between Newtown and Monroe. The towns of Southbury and Monroe, along with Brookfield to the north, Bethel and Redding to the west, and Easton to the south, are Newtown's immediate neighbors.

Whether determined by the retreat of the last great glacier thousands of years ago or by human intervention much more recently, the setting of Newtown is one of beauty and variety. As backdrop, and sometimes as active participant, this scenic design has been an integral part of Newtown's history.

—Mark McGrath

Newtown's Pre-Colonial Residents: Civilizations on a Collision Course

One hundred twenty centuries or so ago, humans first inhabited southern New England. These Paleo-Indians were hunter-wanderers whose prey included mastodon and mammoth, caribou and musk ox.

As the giant animals disappeared and the climate warmed, the early archaic people apparently adapted to their slowly changing environment. They supplemented their food supplies with seasonably available plants, nuts, and acorns and learned to fish and to hunt smaller game such as deer and bear.

By 2000 B.C. residents of the area ranged out from semi-permanent encampments. They stored winter food supplies, quarried chert and quartz for tools, and developed trade routes. It was the woodland Indian descendants of these prehistoric people that European explorers and fishermen first encountered along the New England coast in the 1500s.

The Indians of our area were linked to the other pre-colonial cultures whose territory ranged from Nova Scotia to North Carolina. All the peoples of this part of

"As the ice melted. . . the tundra spread into southern New England followed by herds [of game] and small bands of nomadic Paleo-Indian hunters."

North America have been designated as Eastern Algonquins because of their related languages. What would later become the southern New England states of Massachusetts, Rhode Island, and Connecticut was home to many Indian cultures, including the Paugussett, whose four tribes occupied the lower Housatonic River valley. One of these four, the Pootatuck tribe, was established in an area that included what is now Newtown and Sandy Hook.

By the 16th century, southern New England's Indians were flourishing. They had well established patterns of life that insured adequate supplies of food and clothing throughout the New England seasons without straining the natural resources of their territory.

A typical Indian settlement in the area would include a central, semi-permanent village, frequently located at the junction of two waterways. Such a village was once situated at the confluence of the Housatonic and Pootatuck Rivers. Here a tribe or band (a few hundred people organized into extended kinship relationships and led by a chief or *sachem*) would spend the colder months from November until mid or late March. Shelters that could accommodate 40 to 50 residents were built on a semi-permanent basis here. Each of 10 to 20 of these dwellings might measure up to 100 feet long by 30 feet wide. Hunting parties (exclusively male) would range out from the village to smaller, temporary hunting camps as needed to provide sustenance for the winter.

Gender determined much of the division of labor in the society. The men's activities usually took them away from the village for hunting or navigating the rivers and rapids for fishing — the more dangerous occupations. Intermittently intensive, their work involved a greater risk of death or injury than that of the women, who raised, gathered, and prepared food. Women's work was less intense, but it was continuous and centered near the village and homesteads, most likely in order to facilitate child rearing.

From spring until late autumn, families dispersed to individual farmsteads, which were located for maximum agricultural potential. For the local Pootatucks, one such farmstead most likely was situated near the center of present-day Newtown. Here, women set up wigwams — round, dome-shaped shelters fashioned from grass mats over wooden frames that were designed so that the mats could be removed and the whole camp relocated in a few hours.

Women and children planted and took care of the fields, using light tools that could easily be transported to other sites or just as readily abandoned and replaced at need. Crops in one field might include corn, beans, squash, and pumpkins in a

"Middle Archaic bands gathered at base camps for seasonal fish runs. . . .The continuously rising sea invaded Long Island Sound."

dense tangle of edible vegetation.

After the crops were sown and the plants tended until they could conquer weeds on their own, groups of women and children could leave the farmsteads for two to three months. They picked up their houses and transferred to special-purpose camps for gathering the fruits of summer. The agenda would likely include a stay on Long Island Sound where seafood, cattails, and useful shells could be collected.

While the women were raising the crops and gathering plants, the men of the tribe took on warm weather responsibilities of fishing and hunting. They established camps and erected dams on the rivers for catching spawning runs, spent days hollowing out the local chestnut trees to build heavy dugout canoes for fishing, and went off on extended hunting trips.

This was the well-defined and efficient style of life that local Indians enjoyed when they first made contact with small numbers of European explorers and fishermen. These first encounters would have given few hints of the disaster that lay ahead for the New England natives.

An apparent strength that was to prove a weakness that hurried the downfall of the local Indians was their freedom from disease. Experts detail several possible reasons for the good health of the native population: they resided in areas of relatively low population densities, they kept no domestic animals that could carry or host diseases, and their ancestors had survived in a semi-arctic environment that would have filtered out germs. Whatever the reason, generations of these people had had no immunity whatsoever to the ordinary childhood or more lethal diseases carried by Europeans.

It has been estimated that a native population (in western Connecticut and central Long Island) of nearly 25,000 during the 1500s was reduced to 1,200 individuals by the mid 1600s. Smallpox, measles, and the many other diseases introduced by colonial settlers killed up to 95% of the native population of western Connecticut. In fact, this unintentional reduction in the numbers of Indians was by far the colonists' most devastating and effective means of eliminating competition for the land.

It is not difficult to understand why local Indians offered little trouble to the early citizens of Newtown. Native patterns of living had been drastically altered by sheer loss of numbers; traditional hierarchies of kinship and authority would have been severely disrupted. Physically and socially, these people were at their most vulnerable when the strong and determined European colonists arrived.

The clash of cultures was just beginning. Settlers with their European standards found Indian ways bewildering and often interpreted what they saw inaccurately. Diaries of the settlers mentioned the apparently unplanned and disorganized

Two thousand years ago woodland Indians had developed permanent villages, made pottery, hunted with the bow and developed overland trail systems.

"mess" of Indian crop planting. Although offensive to English eyes, this system actually produced high yields per acre and discouraged weed growth while minimizing depletion of the soil's nutrients.

The apparently wasteful, semi-annual burning of forest land also puzzled the colonists. What they did not realize was that these fast burning, low heat ground fires kept the forest clear of underbrush and thus facilitated hunting and travel. There were more subtle ecological benefits as well. Forest nutrients were replenished more rapidly, creating good growing conditions for gatherable foods such as berries. In addition, the fires made for ideal "edge" habitats that promoted increasing populations of the wildlife species hunted by the Indians.

Encountered mostly at leisure in their semi-permanent villages, the men of the tribe were thought to be lazy and willing to let the women do the hard work. Based on their experience in Europe, the colonists viewed hunting and fishing as leisure activities and did not recognize that the game brought in by men provided skins for clothing the inhabitants in addition to supplying a significant portion of the village's food.

Another circumstance that heightened misunderstanding between the two cultures was a widely differing view of land use and "ownership." Moving from one spot to another throughout the year may have suited the Indian's lifestyle perfectly, but this habit was widely misinterpreted by the colonists. Land apparently unused and uninhabited for much of the year was obviously free to be settled.

Many Indians believed that "selling" the land meant sharing the right to use it. They little expected the permanent dwellings and exclusive claims on sections of the land for cultivation that colonists took for granted. History has made clear both the tragedy and inevitability of the outcome: with so much at stake, the faction stronger in numbers and healthier in bodies quickly prevailed.

The surviving Indians of Newtown and Sandy Hook by the mid-18th century had formed small groups and moved elsewhere, many gravitating to Scatacook in Kent. Although little or nothing was left of their villages or culture, they did leave behind trails that would become the roads and highways of Newtown.

New settlers would also retain part of the Indians' language. The name Connecticut was derived from an Algonquin phrase: "Conne" (long), "tic" (tidal river), "ut" (by). The Housatonic River was called after the Indian "haus-aug-ton-uk," which meant "waterway from the mountain place;" and the local waterway was still the Pootatuck — for the tribe whose name referred to "the country above the falls."

—Carole Telfair and Judith Ince Craven

"Ninety percent of Connecticut's Indians died as a result of diseases brought by European settlers."

Margin Information from *"Indians of Southern New England,"* a chart by Marianne Pfeiffer.

photograph by Jim Bird

10

photograph by David Kriger

part 1

The Eighteenth Century

Weathervane, Sandy Hook

photograph by Joseph I. Kugielsky

The 18th Century
Creating a Tradition

T
he tide of colonial settlement in New England was raging during the 17th Century. The Connecticut Colony was established in 1632 by a group from New Town, later Cambridge, in Massachusetts, who followed Thomas Hooker westward through the wilderness and settled on the shore of the broad and beautiful Connecticut River. They called their colony Newtown. Some years later that town officially became Hartford. Our Newtown was chartered by the General Court (general assembly) of Connecticut Colony in 1708 in the territory then known as Quanneapague.

For a long time many have assumed that Newtown's colonial history began in 1705, when three speculators from Stratford purchased (without the required permit from the general assembly) the Indian lands that eventually became a town.

Actually, the public records of Connecticut Colony reveal that assignment of property here began at least as early as 1667. In that year, the general assembly granted "Mr. Sherman, Mr. Fayrechild, Lt. Curtice, Ens. Judson, Mr. Hawley, & Mr. John Minor liberty to purchase Potatuke and the lands adjoyneing, to be reserved for a village or plantation." Although the original deed has been lost, later documents refer to Samuel Sherman's purchase of a tract which contained a farm owned by Cowanock, a Pootatuck.

The records for May of 1687 state that the court granted to "Mr. Samuel Sherman, Junr., two hundred acres of land out of his father's purchase of the Indians of a mile square." Benjamin Sherman inherited a part of "Cowanock's" farm in 1700. It was bounded by what would be Queen Street on the west, Church Hill Road on the north, the Pootatuck River on the east and probably Mile Hill Road on the south. Thus "Sherman's Old Farm," as it came to be known, encompassed much of what later became the center of Newtown.

Six other grants were made in the Quanneapague territory before 1705. For example, in 1678, the court in Hartford granted to "John Hubbell in Consideration of his loss of one of his fingers and one ear, etc., one hundred acres of land." The familiar names of Botsford and Shelton were also among those of the earliest grant holders.

The legally questionable purchase of 1705 has been a more clearly documented milestone in the establishment of Newtown. William Junos (James), a yeoman, and Captain Samuel Hawley, Jr., were Stratford men. Justus Bush was a mariner from New York. On July 25 (old calendar), 1705, these men met with three sachems of the Pootatuck tribe, Mauquash, Massumpas, and Nunnawauk, at the Indian encampment at the junction of the Housatonic and Pootatuck Rivers.

Acting without the aforementioned authority of the colonial court, which alone had the power to give title, the three speculators bought from the Indians "a Certain Tract of land Butted and Bounded by Stratford, Fairfield, Danbury, New Milford, and the Great River . . .," an area about eight miles long and six miles wide. The deed is recorded in the land records of Newtown. The purchase price was "four guns, four broadcloth Coats, four blankitts, four ruffelly Coats, four Collars, ten shirts, ten pair of stockings, forty pounds of lead, ten pounds of powder and forty knives."

The colonial court was, predictably, not pleased with the transaction and recommended that Junos, Hawley, and

"The Oldest House in Newtown"
1 Poorhouse Road

Local legend states that Daniel Crofut built this house in 1691 and thus has labelled it the oldest house still standing in Newtown. There is, however, reason to question the accuracy of such an early construction date. A recent appraisal by Professor Abbott Cummings of Yale, an expert on antique houses, estimates a more realistic early 1700s origin for the present structure.

The house stands on part of what was an original land grant from William and Mary, and there is reason to believe that some building —perhaps even some part of the existing house— stood there as early as 1691.

For more than 40 years, artists Harrie and Marni Woods owned the house. They and subsequent owners have taken pains to preserve the Colonial details and atmosphere of the house and surroundings. Dr. Stephen Herman and his wife, actress Joan Grant, purchased the property in 1989. They had the central chimney (which vents five fireplaces) rebuilt and have maintained an extensive rose garden on the grounds.

Bush be prosecuted. By May of 1706, Junos had apparently offered to surrender to the court his holdings in the deal. As the other two parties made satisfactory restitution, all three of the land dealers escaped without further penalty.

Before long, Junos sold out part of his interest. Samuel Hawley, however, was apparently more confident of the value of the tract in which he still held a third portion. He joined with other Stratford citizens and bought out Junos' remaining claim and all that of Bush.

In the year 1708, upon petition of 36 settlers a charter was granted, bestowing town rights upon the community. The area was officially defined, and it was decreed that it "shall be one entire town, called by the name of Newtown."

The general assembly appointed a committee to survey the tract and lay out the appropriate number and size of plots. Town boundaries were determined to be Queen Street and Carcass Lane (much later Wendover Road) on the east, Deep Brook on the south, "The Great Hill" toward the west, and the road to Danbury on the north. Within these boundaries, 41 home lots of four acres each were originally laid out.

The original petitioners, along with seven recipients of earlier grants, were the first proprietors of Newtown. Each of the proprietors had the right to "pitch" (draw straws) for the home lots and for other divisions of the common land as soon as they could be laid out. Distribution by this method was construed as "leaving the judgement to God." Proprietors' rights to the land could then be bought, sold, or divided repeatedly.

In the early spring of 1710, 22 Stratford men holding rights to the land "took their pitch" for lots farther from the center of town. Acreage was "equally divided to each proprietor by a Sizer, and what is wanting in quality to be made up in quantity." Most of these lots consisted of 20 acres.

As each division of land was made —even farther removed from the original town plot— notice was given to all inhabitants, and it was voted that any proprietor who disagreed with the arrangement would lose his "pitch." Notifications for such town gatherings were posted "at three certain places ten days before sd meeting, namely at ye oak tree near Sargeant Joseph Botsford, one at ye pound, and one at ye oak tree near Johnathan Booth's house which shall be sufficient warning to ye inhabitants of Newtown." "Pitching" continued for many years, until all the common land had been allocated.

Land was the primary interest of each individual. Swamp land was considered even more valuable than upland, because winter hay could be cut there. Meadows had been kept cleared by the Indian custom of burning. Another method of making brushy land fit for meadow use was to "drown" it. This killed the tree growth and in time the land could be reclaimed for pasture or crops. What was too rocky for plowing was used for sheep pasturage.

Since a man's land was his very existence, boundary lines were of great importance. Disputes were common and were taken very seriously by the townspeople.

Newtown was flourishing in 1723 when a Pootatuck Indian named Quiomph appeared before the town leaders and announced that he was the owner of a tract of land in Sandy Hook which had not been included, as far as he was concerned, in any of the earlier purchases. By that time there were 51 proprietors of the town, and among them they bought the tract from Quiomph for £16.

The first of several disputes with other towns over Newtown's boundaries occurred with Stratford in 1725. A committee was appointed by the court to meet with a similar body from Stratford. If no agreement could be reached, the committee was then authorized to appoint "three uninterested gentlemen" to arbitrate. The boundary was mutually agreed upon in 1725, but was not finally confirmed by Connecticut's general court until 1761, when a line officially distinguished Newtown from what later became the independent towns of Monroe and Trumbull.

The boundary on the opposite end of town also caused friction. By 1731, New Milford brought legal action against Newtown for "neglecting to perambulate ye line," and Capt. Thomas Tousey was appointed to represent Newtown before the Superior Court in New Haven. In December of 1734, the controversy was satisfactorily settled.

With the original purchase of 1705, Brookfield (as it later became) was included in the boundaries of Newtown. About 1751, the inhabitants of the "West Farm" and "Whiskenere" sections expressed their desire to join Danbury and New Milford to form an Ecclesiastical Society. (After all, they were very far from the Meeting House in the center of Newtown village.) However, Newtown presented powerful opposition in the general assembly and conceded only that the north end citizens need not pay to support the Newtown minister, provided that they would take care of one in their own district. They engaged the Reverend Thomas Brooks, who developed so large and so devoted a following that the parish — first called "Newbury" (combining in its name *New*town and *New* Milford with Dan*bury*) — preferred to consider itself "Brook's field," the origin of its later town name. The disagreements continued until 1788, when Newtown relinquished its claim and the parish of Newbury was incorporated as the town of Brookfield.

In 1758, the usual committees were formed yet again to "perambulate, renew and erect ye boundaries" between Danbury and Newtown. As in other disputes, the boundaries referred to often consisted of piles of stones, natural or manmade ditches, or landmark trees.

Apparently residents in some of the disputed areas used the boundary squabbles to advantage. Tradition holds that Dodgingtown came by its name because it lay within the area which for a long time was claimed by both Newtown and Danbury. When the Newtown tax collectors appeared, the citizens claimed vehemently that they were Danbury residents; when the Danbury agents turned up, everybody insisted that they were Newtowners! Nothing could be proven while the boundaries were undetermined, so the dodging continued successfully for a number of years. This section of Danbury later became Bethel.

Government: A Town is Formed

The year 1711 is a momentous one in Newtown's history. It was then that the general court of Connecticut Colony granted the settlement the power to elect its own officers and to enjoy all the rights and privileges of other towns in the state.

The first business meeting was held at the house of Peter Hubbell on September 24, 1711. Hubbell was voted Newtown's first Town Clerk, Abraham Kimberly constable, Ebenezer Prindle and Thomas Sharp surveyors of highways, Joseph Gray and Daniel Foote fence viewers, and Johnathan Booth field driver or hayward.

The general court appointed the "number 7 to be ye town Brand Mark for their horses," and also decreed that the annual town meeting should be held in December. Consequently, on the following December 4th, at the house of Daniel Foote, the inhabitants met and elected Ebenezer Pringle as First Selectman, with Samuel Sanford and John Platt "Townsmen" for the year. Also elected were "listers and collectors," a "brander of horses," and a committee of five to lay out divisions of land and highways.

It was moreover enacted that "all persons who refuse or neglect to attend ye town meetings shall pay ye sum of three shillings to ye treasury of ye town."

Another government duty which had to be dealt with was providing a burial place for the dead. Accordingly, on March 24, 1711, one and a half acres in the lower part of the community were set aside as a town burial ground. This southerly or "old" section of the Newtown Village Cemetery, was located near the center of town on what became Elm Drive opposite Hawley Road.

In the town record of 1711, it was voted for "Stephen Pearmelee to have the use of one and a half acres, which is the burying place or yard provided he clear the bushes and fences it and sows it with English grass seed." Provision for further care

Jeremiah Northrupp
Peter Hubbell
Jonathan Hubbell
Thomas Bennitt
Jonathan Booth
Benjamin Dunning
Ephriam Osborne
Freegrace Adams
Moses Johnson
Abraham Kimberly
Samuel Ferris
Ebenezer Johnson
Samuel Sanford
Josiah Bennitt
Thomas Toucey [or Tousey]
John Lake
Jeremiah Turner
Mr. Tousey
Thomas Sharp's heirs
Joseph Gray
Capt. Halley [or Hawley]
Capt. Curtis
Ebenezer Booth
John Platt
Eleazer Morris
Joseph Bristol
Stephen Parmalee

was made in 1769, when it was voted that "Mr. John Chandler shall have the liberty to fence the burying ground for pasture so long as he will keep it in good fence."

The cemetery was very far from the people living in the northwest part of the village, so, in 1848, they presented a petition to the Selectmen asking for "60 rods for a burying place" of their own. This was the Land's End Cemetery in Hawleyville off Whisconier Hill toward Brookfield on Route 25. Jeremiah Turner who, according to tradition, was the first white child born in Newtown, was buried there, as was the renowned Dr. Thomas Brooks.

The next cemetery was established in the opposite part of the growing settlement, in Zoar, and was a private enterprise. In 1767, Samuel Adams sold an acre and a half out of the lands of the great Zoar farm to a group of citizens of the district. Three years later the town voted "that the farm called Zoar shall have the old bury-

photograph by William R. Greene

Stone rubbing is a popular 20th century activity at Newtown's Village Cemetery.

photograph by Mark McGrath

ing cloth, and that the selectmen shall proceed to procure a new one for the use of the town." This referred to the pall which was draped over the dead when, often to be interred without coffins, they were carried on farm wagons to their graves.

The Taunton cemetery, made up by two purchases of land totalling 64 square rods, was set aside in 1787, on Taunton Hill Road. That same year, the Hunting-town cemetery was also established. Forty-eight square rods of ground were sold "for the sole purpose of a burying ground so long as it should be used for that purpose."

Welfare problems were not unknown to 18th century governments. Many instances of providing for the poor and needy and the aged and infirm were noted in early town records. For example, Samuel Hendrix, in 1745, was released from paying taxes for a year in consideration of his providing for his aged mother. Arrangements were made to pay anyone 16 shillings a week each for caring for Thadeus and Pheneas Lyon, "Idiots or Distracted men."

Tax collection was another major duty of government. Rates seem to have been high. Samuel Sherman, for instance, made brooms and was taxed $150.00 on the assessed valuation of his business. Oxen, horses, and sheep were all taxed. Of course, the land was the chief source of town revenue, but poll taxes of $30.00 were levied on citizens 18 to 20 years of age, and $60.00 on those 21 to 70 years old. Houses, chimneys, window panes, fireplaces, mirrors, watches — all were taxable. At one time even the churches were assessed and taxed.

Religion: The Established Church and Dissent

By tradition, religion was virtually indistinguishable from government to the American colonists. One of the first duties of the town founders was to secure the services of a minister — a non-conformist of Presbyterian (later the term "Congregationalist" was used) persuasion. Accordingly, at the first town meeting it was "voted to invite Mr. Phineas Fisk for six months trial as minister to settle among us."

Records indicate that Mr. Fisk was difficult to convince. Despite the towns-people's efforts, this minister (actually still a student) never did come to Newtown. In April of 1713, the town authorized Ebenezer Smith to go all the way to Weth-ersfield to "treat with Mr. Thomas Tousey and request him to preach a Sabbath or two with us." A month later, the town voted to pay 30 pounds salary and to plant Mr. Tousey's home lot in exchange for a year of ministry. By November, Mr. Tousey was asked to fill the position "as long as God shall grant him life and health."

Erecting a meeting house for religious services was next on the town agenda. This was undertaken in the fall of 1713, when a committee was appointed and the members were authorized to hire workmen and put up a 32 by 40 foot building.

Something evidently went wrong, because it was not until 1718 that Thomas Scidmore offered to build the meeting house for 45 pounds. It was agreed in 1719, that "where the lane that runs easterly and westerly intersects the maine town street that runs northerly and southerly shall be ye place to set ye meeting house for carrying on ye public worship of God." Until the building was finished, religious services were held in people's homes, and the owners were properly compensated by the town.

All inhabitants were taxed for support of the church and attendance was compulsory. Punishment for absence was a fine of five shillings or an hour in the stocks.

The building, when completed, was very simple, unheated and with little light. Plain board benches served as seats. Observance of Sunday was an all-day affair with both morning and afternoon services and long sermons. An interval of one and a quarter hours at noon provided some relief and led to the establishment of "Sabbath Day Houses."

These unique features of colonial life were snug little buildings which the town permitted citizens from a distance to erect along the highways near the meeting house. During the interval permitted between morning and afternoon services, families retired to these small houses. Usually divided into separate sections for men and women, they provided warmth and the opportunity for rest and for partaking of a meal brought from home. Some were used in common among friends, others were strictly family affairs.

Over the years repairs and alterations were made in the meeting house, but it was a long while before the board benches gave way to "fationable pews" and the gallery stairs and floor were laid. By 1746, we find the parishioners repairing the gables and adding a "bell free." A little later a tax of 12 pence on the pound was levied for further finishing the galleries.

In 1762, Captain Amos Botsford and Lt. Nathaniel Briscoe promised to acquire and pay for a bell for the steeple. The bell marked a great innovation in town, because, until its installation, people had been summoned to church services and public meetings by Stephen Parmalee and his drum. The ringing of the new bell subsequently brought Newtowners to the meeting house, the town house, or to any public gathering. The drummer was thus replaced by Abel Botsford, who "should be bellringer for ye year ensuing, and shall have for his services for ringing ye bell and sweeping ye meeting house, 40 shilling a year."

The old Congregational Church building and the liberty pole are central features of Newtown's 20th century Main Street.

photograph by Ken Kast

When the bell was later re-cast and hung again, the Church of England society contributed nearly a fifth of the cost, and an inscription read: "The Gift of Capt. Amos Botsford and Lt. Briscoe, 1768."

The established church, along with other town government institutions, encountered difficulties and controversy in the 18th century. In fact, in 1724, after 11 years in Newtown, Mr. Thomas Tousey, the town's first minister, was invited to quit his post because "Ye Major part of ye inhabitants could not sit easy under him."

The minister called to follow Mr. Tousey was the Reverend Mr. John Beach, a young man from Stratford who came to be very popular among his parishioners. About 1732, Mr. Beach evidently became unsure in his own mind of the validity of ordination in the Congregational Church and resigned his parish. The town records of the time show clearly the distress of the townspeople. Firm in his convictions, Mr. Beach left home and family, sailed for the mother country, and was ordained in the Church of England.

There was a powerful aristocratic contingent in early Connecticut which remained loyal to the Church of England as it did later to the Tory viewpoint in political affiliations. However, the established church of the colony, which everyone was required to support by taxation, regardless of personal faith, was the Congregational denomination. Nothing could have been more disruptive to the peaceful life of the community than to have this well-loved clergyman change his allegiance.

This action caused bitter personal confrontation with some of the less tolerant townspeople when Mr. Beach returned as a Church of England missionary to the Newtown and Redding area. According to tradition, he was greatly harassed by some of his former parishioners.

Despite this controversy, the first service of the Church of England conducted by Mr. Beach took place under an immense buttonball tree near the corner of Main Street and Glover Avenue. A tablet later marked the site, and tradition states that the first Episcopal church in town was located near this spot. The building 28 by 24 foot, was framed, raised, and enclosed on a Saturday. The following day, the workers assembled for services "sitting on timbers and kneeling on the ground."

A second church was named Trinity Episcopal and erected in 1746, farther up the street on the west side. Near the end of the 18th century, the Episcopalians were granted permission to move the Congregational meeting house across the street and to build for themselves a new church at the corner of Main Street and Church Hill Road.

The move of the Congregational meeting house occurred on June 13, 1792. In eight and a half hours, the building, steeple and all, was moved a distance of eight rods to the opposite side of Main Street.

Although these two institutions were the major religious influence on 18th century Newtown, there were other denominations that, at least for a time, appeared on the scene. A Sandemanian Society had a considerable effect on town affairs for about 50 years. These followers of the Scotsman Robert Sandeman organized here about 1740 to hold their services or "love feasts" in each other's houses. This emotional type of evangelism drew many members away from the more austere Congregational and Episcopal churches, but the movement died out before 1800. The first Baptist Church in the area was established at Zoar Corners, where, in 1794, the society erected a large barn-like structure.

Education: the Development of the Districts

Newtown's preference for economical, multi-use buildings was evidenced as early

as the 18th century, when townspeople recognized the possibility of meeting two needs with one structure. On October 9, 1717, it was voted that a combined school and town house should be built on the main street. The building was used as both for 16 years.

Those who could not pay the school tax of two pence a pound on their estates were permitted to turn in the equivalent value in wheat, rye, corn, etc. The Selectmen were authorized to engage a schoolmaster "so long as ye overplus money in ye Town rate will support it." Teacher employment terms increased from three months to four, five or six, and were supported partly by the town and partly by the "schoolers," or by private subscription.

Geographical size and population growth of the village created a demand for a second schoolhouse at the north end of town by 1726. Soon, as the far-flung settlement continued to grow, more school districts were established. Each had a local committee to direct the building and administration of each school and the hiring of a teacher. Each committee also reflected the unique character of the district and its inhabitants — unfortunately, not always to the benefit of education policy. As was to be expected, children's education in Newtown showed as much diversity as its separate districts did.

The following list records the founding of the various districts: Taunton in 1738,

photograph/detail preceeding page by Mary Mitchell

Above and opposite, the Middle Gate School house, 1850.

Zoar in 1745, Land's End (Whiskenear) in 1745, Palestine in 1748, Hanover in 1755, South Center (Kettletown, later Tinkerfield) in 1761, Deep Brook in 1767, Slut's Hill (Mt. Pleasant) in 1768, Lake George (perhaps a combination of the names of two residents, Lake and George) in 1768, Flat Swamp in 1769, Pohtatuck (Sandy Hook) in 1779, Bear Hills in 1783, Gray's Plain in 1784, Head o' Meadow in 1784, Wapping in 1786, Half Way River (originally known as Ragged Corner) in 1786, Gregory's Orchard in 1788, Walker's Farms (later part of Monroe) in 1789, Toddy Hill (Botsford) in 1789, and Huntingtown in 1794. Occasionally, districts united, split, changed names, or were added until the advent of town-wide consolidation in the 20th century, at which time there still were more than 20 school districts.

Schoolhouses in the early colonial years had only fireplaces for heat. The value of firewood was deducted from the tuition of the student providing it, and when it wasn't provided, school closed.

Around the walls was a sharply sloping shelf which was used as a desk, too steep to keep the books from sliding off. Ranged in front of this, with backs to the teacher, the pupils sat on hard wooden benches too high for the feet of most children to rest on the floor. Drinking water often had to be fetched in a bucket from the nearest farm, and one dipper was shared by everyone.

The schools were under the over-all management of the Selectmen. Many sources besides town taxes were drawn upon for school support — even liquor licenses. A boon was granted in 1795, when the Connecticut State School Fund was established. This revenue was realized by the sale of state-owned lands in the Western Reserve in Ohio. The territory had been claimed from the Crown by Connecticut under her charter of 1642, which granted to the state land "limited East and West by the Sea." Proceeds of the sale were distributed among the towns for purposes of funding education.

With this state aid, the Newtown School Society was formed in 1796. For the first time, the Selectmen were relieved of much of the burden of school administration. The Society acted as an overall authority endeavoring to insure some measure of consistency in the fragmented school system of Newtown for some 40 years.

The Taunton Schoolhouse

This little building has had a long and useful life. First built in 1738 as the first outlying school in Newtown, it was in active use as an educational center for nearly two centuries. When the town sold several of its old one room schoolhouses in 1950, a neighboring landowner on Taunton Hill Road purchased and looked out for the empty building.

Twenty-five years later, John Vouros, a single schoolteacher living in the owners' home across the street, was very taken with the old school. When he married, he and his wife Jane, both on the faculty at Newtown Middle School, bought the building and some of the surrounding land. In 1975 they had the schoolhouse moved back on the property, designed the interior, and lived in it as a one room house.

When the Vouros' needed more space, an unusual expansion project look form. With their own plans and the help of an architect, John and Jane Vouros added 11 rooms onto the one room — maintaining the character of an 18th century schoolhouse as the focal point of a modern suburban home.

photograph by Ken Kast

the needs of an egalitarian rural population. Crafters remained loyal to the styles of the coastal communities in which they had been trained. Woods used were mostly local varieties: cherry, oak, whitewood, pine, maple, and birch.

The chairs constructed by craftsmen like the

Booths and the Prindles were referred to in the inventories by names such as "plain," "round-top," and "fiddleback" chairs. The elements of construction were generally "turned" (shaped on a lathe to be fit into drilled holes), a fast and easy method of manufacture that produced a good looking yet relatively inexpensive piece. Seats were commonly of the "flag" (or woven) variety. Chairs like the "round-top" (also called the "York" style) and "fiddleback" allowed a measure of decorative style that became the

country version of furniture popular at that time in American cities.

Newtown's early citizens generally resisted the newer "market economy." They lived, worked, and socialized in town, and, whenever possible, bought or bartered for their household necessities at home. This traditional outlook is reflected today in what they left behind — even something as commonplace as a kitchen chair.

Chairs representative of those manufactured in Newtown; courtesy of the Cyrenius H. Booth Library Collection.

photographs by Joseph I. Kugielsky

Throughout the 1700s Newtown remained to a large extent economically isolated. Farmland was most often passed from father to sons. Land owners with familiar names like Briscoe, Ferris, Peck, Parmalee, and Prindle increasingly encouraged their children to develop craftsmen skills so that, by 1900, Newtown was to a great extent self-sufficient.

Nevertheless, there was some economic diversity. Zibah Blakeslee had a gold and silver smithing business on Main Street. In 1764, a mining venture was undertaken by a number of citizens of Sandy Hook. They leased the cliffs of Rocky Glen to a New York prospector for 40 years, with permission "if need be, to dig to the center of the earth." There were no profitable results.

Newtown had a number of slave owners. In 1756, there were 23 slaves in town, and we know that, as early as 1735, slaves were held here. They were listed and valued in records like household effects. Whether slaves were farm hands or house servants was not recorded. Eighteenth century anti-slavery sentiments were not popular in much of Fairfield County, but slave holding was not widespread. The last reference in Newtown to slave ownership occurred in 1804.

Sugar Lane Colonial

photograph by Ken Kast

This 1750 colonial on Sugar Lane was once the center of a thriving dairy operation know as Briary Hill Farm. For many years it was owned by Miss Zaina Patterson, a New York actress known for her performance in "The Dollar Princess" at the Chestnut Street Opera House. She also performed at the Globe Street Theater on Broadway.

When her acting career came to an end, Miss Patterson regularly drove her own truck into New York to sell milk and fresh corn to Schraft's and other restaurants in the theater district.

The house and part of the farm were purchased in the 1970s by David and Eleanor Zolov.

The Revolutionary War

The residents of a quiet country town like Newtown must have had difficulty comprehending the tragedy of the impending Revolutionary War. Although most towns and counties in Connecticut had, by late 1774, expressed opposition to British rule, Newtown still pondered. A March 6, 1775 "memorial" (communication) sent to the general assembly wondered whether the conflict between England and the colonies might not be a simple misunderstanding or even a jest. In 1770, half of the 350 families in town were members of the Church of England and had, through the years, remained in touch with the homeland.

In 1774 and 1775, the town government and Newtown's two members of the general assembly were still loyal to the King. The assembly ousted one of them, and the other resigned. In October, 1776, Newtown had no representation at the general court in New Haven. There was a blank space after the town's name in the record.

The previous July the Declaration of Independence had been signed, so the legislative session opened in a mood of dark solemnity. Questions of great importance requiring drastic action were likely to arise. The assembly passed a resolution approving the Declaration of Independence and created an act prescribing and adjuring an oath of fidelity to the state. Every office-holder and unindentured man (freeman) in Connecticut was obliged to take the oath before he was received as an elector. Newtown was conspicuous by its absence of representation at the 1777 general assembly session.

Newtowners were slow to pledge fidelity. Between August 25, 1777, when eight men ventured forth to swear allegiance before the Town Clerk, and April 12, 1790, when the record was closed, only 337 townspeople took the oath.

By 1778, however, Newtown had three representatives present and voting at the general assembly. Each approved every one of the Articles of Confederation which had been forwarded by Congress to the state. By unanimous vote of the general assembly, the state delegates were instructed to voice approval in the Congress.

The same year, the general assembly cited acts of insubordination among three companies in the first society of Newtown's 16th regiment. The chief officer of the regiment was empowered to warn the local companies to meet and select appropriately qualified and loyal officers or forfeit the right of selection to the civil authorities of the town.

Meanwhile, a change in local government, if not a change of heart, had been accomplished with some pressure from the general assembly and at the request of Governor John Trumbull. Local committees of "safety" were established to launch a

STEVEN KELLOGG

series of vigilante-type actions against British supporters. Townspeople had moved from an attitude of perplexity to one of ferocity, as conflicts erupted between neighbors and friends, and even within families.

Tories, or Loyalists as they preferred to be called, were continuously tormented by bands of patriots who roamed the countryside at night. Aunt Mary Ann Glover, who died in 1878 at the age of 102, recalled a family legend that her Tory father would hide in the woods when expecting a raid. On one such occasion, the Whig marauders, finding him abed, amused themselves by pricking him with their bayonets. They helped themselves to Mrs. Glover's pumpkin pies and tossed a piece to the dog, whereupon the lady of the house remarked contemptuously that the pies were good enough for the likes of them, but not fit for the dog.

Only 20 years earlier, during the French and Indian War, Newtown had received and supported a French family driven into exile from Nova Scotia by the British. Now many of the town's Tory families were forced to flee to Canada or to Long Island, both held by the British. In January of 1777, residents of Newfield Harbor (Bridgeport) petitioned for harbor guards to "hinder the Tories of Newtown from communicating freely with their brethren on Long Island. . ." As the Tories left or were ordered out of town, their property was confiscated and turned over to the state.

One British sympathizer who did not leave was John Beach, minister of Trinity Church in Newtown and Christ Church in Redding. Though he was threatened with execution, he continued to pray for the King at his Sunday services. In 1781, six months before his death at the age of 82, he wrote of his pride in members of his congregation who had refused to comply with the doings of the new national government.

Robert Thompson, on the other hand, was a Tory not destined to live such a long life. He was hanged in Newtown on June 9, 1777, for "recruiting, spying, and treasonable practices."

The tales retold of violence and cruelty expressed and reflected the fear and desperation which was felt on both sides. An entry in the journal of Clermont Crevecoeur, a French artillery officer who traveled through Newtown on June 28, 1781, illustrated that patriots had reason to fear the Tories:

The Town of Newtown is in the province of New York [sic]. We saw much poverty there among the inhabitants, as well as ruined fields and houses. This is the capital of the Tory country, and as you may well imagine, we took great precautions to protect ourselves from their acts of cruelty. They usually strike

photographs by Ken Kast

Hillbrow, or Head O' Main Street

Rumors of a ghostly presence in the house known as Hillbrow on Main Street date back to the Revolutionary War, when a Tory resident in the house was allegedly harrassed to his death by hungry French soldiers.

Tradition holds that some of Rochambeau's troops took exception to the vocal loyalist contingent they found in Newtown. Tormented by the smell of baking bread that Hillbrow's owner withheld from the visiting army, the angry Frenchmen pulled an elderly man from the house and chased him up and down Main Street. The man died from effects of the ordeal. Later, his shade settled into the house, presumably in righteous indignation at such treatment.

However, whatever presence has been felt at Hillbrow over the years has been surprisingly benevolent. Although 20th century residents have admitted to an occasional feeling of not being alone in an empty room, puzzling disappearances of household objects, and unusual air currents, no owner of record has experienced fearful or threatening sightings. Resident dogs, however, have reportedly been sensitive to a teasing presence. (See illustration opposite page.)

Head O' Main Street, was built around 1715 by Ebenezer Blackman. This impressive building has long been a Newtown landmark. It remained in the Blackman family for several generations.

Owners Richard and Dorothy Mulligan have preserved a huge early 18th century beehive oven that dominates the central part of the house. Another unusual feature is a curving entry staircase that splits in two directions at the second floor level. Years of settling have created extremely uneven walls and 50 windows that each require a different length of curtain.

by night, when they go out in bands, attack a post, then retire to the woods where they bury their arms. . . These people are very difficult to identify, since an honest man and a scoundrel can look alike.

In April of 1777, Major General William Tryon launched his raid on the city of Danbury. As the British passed through Newtown on their way to the battle, patriot families gathered their valuables and secreted them away. The Fairchilds of Taunton reportedly threw the family silver into a pillowcase and dropped it into a well under the parlor floor, where it remained safely until the soldiers had moved on.

Two years later, the same General Tryon returned to Connecticut, this time to launch a series of attacks on towns along the coastline. On separate raids during the year, his troops burned the towns of Fairfield and Norwalk, sparing only the places of worship and a few homes of avowed Loyalists.

As though hardships of the war were not enough to bear, the town was plagued by recurrent outbreaks of sickness. A severe smallpox epidemic swept the area. Rumors circulated that the disease had been introduced by a party of exchanged prisoners who had been landed at Stratford under a flag of truce. In Stratford alone, 600 people contracted the sickness. In Newtown, a town meeting voted that the town should use its influence to prevent the spread of smallpox "by inoculation or some other method." Later, the inoculation method was "negatived in full and open town meeting."

Life was precarious. Gravestones attest to the numbers of deaths among children and young men and women. Medical treatment was primitive, and the war had rendered food and clothing scarce.

Young soldiers, too, suffered severe deprivation as they poured into the encampment that existed at Redding in 1778 and 1779 under Major Israel Putnam. A volunteer wrote, "we arrived at Redding about Christmas and prepared to build huts for our winter quarters. And now came on . . . the winter campaign of starving." Through the bitter winter, 3,000 troops waited in misery for the British to make their move.

Eight to twelve soldiers were crowded into a primitive 14 by 16 foot hut. One report listed 162 men in a regiment of 434 as "unfit for duty for want of shoes." Peter Fairchild of Newtown, luckier than many, came home to Taunton from camp at Redding to see his mother. While he was home, the women in the family cut and sewed a heavy overcoat from their homespun wool. He returned to camp considerably warmer than his fellow soldiers.

Despite the turbulent Tory problem and despite the poverty and sickness, Newtown did its share in the cause of American freedom. Frequent town meetings were called for the purpose of raising the town's quota of volunteers to fight. Not once did the town have to resort to the draft, and the names of the town's foremost men are on Connecticut's honor roll.

Connecticut's vital contributions of food and supplies during the Revolution earned it the title of "Provision State." Again and again, Newtown contributed its share, though sometimes with difficulty. Supplies of flour, beef, and pork were packed in barrels and forwarded to the forces in the field or deposited at the homes of fatherless families in town.

Sacrifice and suffering notwithstanding, the townspeople persevered. When peace was officially proclaimed on September 3, 1783, Aunt Mary Ann Glover remembered that an ox was roasted whole at the head of Newtown (Main) Street in celebration.

—revision by Carole Telfair of material from *Newtown: Past and Present*, 1975

photograph courtesy of *The Newtown Bee*

Newtown's American Bicentennial re-enactment of the French army's encampment in town included a mock Revolutionary War battle at Newtown High School.

Rochambeau:
The French Army in Newtown

In 1774, even as trouble brewed in Britain's American colonies, the youthful King Louis XVI ascended the proud Bourbon throne of France at the court of Versailles. France hungered to avenge the loss of her Canadian colonies to England in the French and Indian War of 20 years before. Coincidentally, at the start of the Ameri-

can Revolution, Benjamin Franklin of Pennsylvania and Silas Deane of Connecticut had appeared at the French court to appeal for money, arms, and volunteers.

France's most illustrious volunteer for the American cause returned home in 1779 to recount his adventures and to recruit a full division of troops to aid the colonial cause of liberty. The Marquis de LaFayette, 22 years of age, a schoolmate and friend of the King's

younger brother, had been commissioned a Major General in the Army of the United States, had been wounded in the Battle of Brandywine, and had become a close personal friend of General George Washington.

At the King's command, a new expedition was launched on May 2, 1780. The French commander this time was not the impetuous LaFay ette but a proven older general: a man who was to be known as America's overlooked Founding

photographs courtesy of *The Newtown Bee*

Rochambeau's Encampment Re-enacted

The march of Rochambeau's army and its encampment in Newtown were re-enacted twice. First, the event was staged as part of Newtown's celebration of America's bicentennial. Among the "troops" entering town on June 28, 1976, was the Comte Phillippe de Chastellux, a descendant of Major General Francois Jean de Beauvoir Chastellux, nobleman and aide de camp to Rochambeau during the 1781 march.

To mark the 200th anniversary of the American-French alliance that resulted in victory in Virginia, the state of Rhode Island sponsored a re-enactment of the entire march from Newport to Yorktown. The "army" crossed the Housatonic into Newtown on October 11, 1981. Five companies, including the authentic French "Saintonge" troop, took part in this tribute.

Father. His full name was Maréchal Jean-Baptiste de Vimeur, Count de Rochambeau.

From his arrival in July of 1780 until June 1781, Rochambeau and his troops were at Newport, Rhode Island. Although he was criticized in both France and America for keeping his regiments bottled up there, Rochambeau wisely dissuaded Washington from taking a land offensive until the Americans had secured control of the sea.

That time came on June 18, when French troops began to march westward from Providence. In all, Rochambeau's forces consisted of 600 artillery, 600 cavalry, and 3,600 infantry. On the long march, some of the officers set an example by walking the long distances at the head of their regiments.

The inhabitants of the Rhode Island and Connecticut countryside were enthusiastic over the resplendent French Army. The Burbonnais in their black and red uniforms; the Saintonge in white and green; Royal Deux-Ponts in white; and the artillery in blue with red facings, white spatterdashes, and red pompoms; all with hats peaked fore and aft were quite an impressive sight. When the troops reached Hartford, the newspapers were extravagant with their praise for reasons other than dress:

> *A finer body of men was never in arms, and no army was better furnished with everything necessary for a campaign. The exact discipline of the troops, and the attention of the officers to prevent any injury to individuals have made the march of this army through the country very agreeable to the inhabitants; and it is with great pleasure we assure our readers, not a single disagreeable circumstance has taken place.*

39

While these regiments were on the march through Hartford, Farmington, Southington, and Break Neck (Middlebury), the cavalry corps of the Duc de Lauzun was covering the seaward left flank. These troops passed through Derby, crossed the Naugatuck and Housatonic Rivers, and struggled up a steep hill into New Stratford (Monroe). The flanking operation had been well timed, for on the same day, June 28, Rochambeau and his first regiment reached the Housatonic River at Newtown.

Crossing a river was a major operation for any army. Although the Housatonic had a wooden bridge, the heavy equipment had to be forded across. The most difficult pieces were the siege guns and the brass mortars (squat iron buckets weighing four tons each, standing three feet high, and each capable of arching a hundred-pound iron ball high into the air). Eight teams of oxen strained to haul these loads up the further bank of the river.

As the troops and equipment made the crossing, they took the road directly away from the Housatonic River into Newtown, to the camping ground in the meadows southwest of the village.

Why had Newtown been chosen for the 10 day campsite? With a population of 2,400 souls, it was not a large town, but the commissary had reported that provisions could be found there. Flour for bread was ground at the mill on the Pootatuck River. Beef, lamb, and hogs were slaughtered on Carcass Lane, and this meat could be salted to travel for future use.

On the evening of June 28, Count Rochambeau was established in the inn across the road from Newtown's Congregational Church. Intermittently for three days, his troops marched in review past their commander's hostelry.

It had been tentatively planned that Washington would meet Rochambeau at Newtown, and, in fact, the American General had already moved his army from West Point across to the east bank of the Hudson some 50 miles away from the French position. He sent the following dispatch to Rochambeau:

Camp near Peekskill, 27 June, 1781

Sir: I have the honor of receiving your Excellency's favor of the 23rd instant from Hartford. It would have given me the greatest pleasure could I have made it convenient to meet you at Newtown, but independently of many arrangements which are necessary at the first taking of the field, I am detained by the hourly expectation of the Chevalier-de-la-Lauzun. I am pleased to find that your idea of the position which will be proper for the troops under your command coincides with my own and I shall be happy in giving your quarter-master general every assistance in reconnoitering and making out your camp...I am, &c,

George Washington

Because of Washington's delay and an urgent communication requesting that Rochambeau "push on his troops with greater haste than he now intends," the French army broke camp at Newtown on July 1st and proceeded westward to join Washington's army on July 6th at Phillipsburg, New York. Together, the forces of American and Frenchmen marched through New Jersey, Delaware, Maryland, Williamsburg, and on to victory over the British General Cornwallis at Yorktown, Virginia.

Thus, "the march that won the battle that won the war that won the United States freedom" tarried at Newtown, Connecticut.

On June 26, 1954, 173 years later, the Rochambeau Bridge was dedicated. It carried Route 84 across the Housatonic River between Southbury and Newtown.

The Upper Factory, Pootatuck River.

photograph by Mary Mitchell

part II

The Nineteenth Century

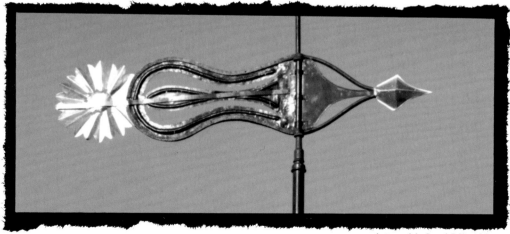

photograph by Joseph I. Kugielsky

This weathervane, now atop Edmond Town Hall on Main Street, once adorned Trinity Episcopal Church.

The 19th Century
Growth Becomes Tradition

*N*ewtown entered the 1800s as an agricultural village. By mid-century, the industrial revolution had arrived, ushering in new prosperity and an ethnic diversity that expanded the political, economic, geographic, and social conditions of the town. Sandy Hook became a vital area, outdistancing economically the quiet Main Street and farms up the hill.

Many aspects of Newtown life, however, did not change despite the new mix of farm and working families who gathered to enjoy long-established winter activities. Skating parties on the Foundry Pond (the ice pond) and races in fast, graceful sleighs remained very popular. A famous sledding party was once held when, with snow conditions exactly right, a group of young men coasted on the road from the top of Mt. Pleasant hill down to the Pootatuck.

Taunton Pond was throughout the century a fisherman's favorite. Steps to regulate the sport there were taken in 1858. In 1870, the pond was stocked with black bass, and no fishing was permitted for the next three years. Trout abounded in the local brooks. Quail and pheasant, rabbits, deer, foxes, opossums, raccoons, and an occasional wildcat provided sport for hunters. A fox hunt of great renown was held in 1875.

Many of the century's social affairs were undertaken with a civic objective — such as raising funds for the John Beach Memorial Library in 1877. Performances of the Dramatic Club helped to build sidewalks, and other events raised money for the volunteer fire company.

Patriotism was another unifying factor that brought the farmers, industrialists, and workers of Newtown together. In 1882 there were two brass bands in town which were called upon frequently, especially at the Fourth of July festivities. These were elaborate all-day affairs, with no restrictions on the use of fireworks.

In the great spirit of national celebration on the occasion of the U. S. centennial year of 1876, Newtown's first Liberty Pole was erected on July 4th. Forty-three citizens raised $107.50 to purchase the pole and flag. (This first flagpole was to be succeeded by a second and a third, always in the same location on Main Street. For years it was painted by Bert Nichols, who shinnied up the pole without benefit of safety ropes, an event which always drew an audience.)

Government: Adapting to the Busy 19th Century

In 1818, Newtown accepted and ratified the "Constitution of civil government of the people of this State." This same Constitution served Connecticut until 1965.

In May of 1824, the Borough of Newtown, the second oldest in the state, was incorporated by the Connecticut general assembly. Thus the approximate geographical center of town became a separate unit with limited self-government powers and officials. At the same time, the borough and its residents retained the full rights and responsibilities of all Newtown districts and citizens.

In response to necessity and sometimes to disaster, the government and townspeople also set about providing services and protective measures against some of the most pressing 19th century dangers.

Fire was an ever-present menace. In 1803, the townspeople voted $100 toward purchasing a fire engine. Two months later the vote was rescinded, and instead Elijah Nichols was appointed "chimney viewer."

In 1807, a serious conflagration on Main Street threatened to wipe out many dwellings. A group led by the Honorable William Edmond raised $450 by private subscription toward the purchase of a fire engine, but it was learned that the cost of "a good and effectual engine with a house to shelter it " would be in the neighborhood of $700.

The group then presented a petition to the Selectmen asking for money to provide an adequate sum. The petition stated that "seriously alarmed at a recent event which threatened for a time to lay their dwellings in ashes, to unhouse their families and produce a scene of destruction and distress awful to contemplate and too painful to describe," the citizens "met to take into consideration their exposed and dangerous situation."

Their unanimous opinion was that the householders were duty bound to see that "their chimneys were swept or cleaned by burning, and that they should provide themselves with ladders as expeditiously as possible." A fire engine was considered to be "the best instrument properly served with which to contend against so unruly and dangerous an element and indeed the only one in which any just confidence of success might be placed in the hour of danger."

A town meeting was called to consider the petition, and $200 from the treasury was voted to augment the $450 already in hand for the purpose, "provided that nothing should subject the town hereafter to the payment of any other or further sum, either for the engine, a house to shelter it, or for cisterns, ladders, fire hooks, ropes, buckets, working the engine or any expense whatever respecting the same, but the town shall be exempted therefrom in the same manner as though this vote had not been passed."

The town seems to have taken no further action in this connection except to appoint annually a chimney viewer, a post held for years by the same Elijah Nichols. However, benefits for the Fire Company became regular social events and were supported by the townspeople.

Thus was founded the Newtown Hook and Ladder, the oldest fire fighting company in Newtown. Early in its history the company raised funds to buy a fire engine. Each member of the company was expected to provide buckets and ladders.

On May 1, 1883, a committee recommended, and it was passed, that the sum of $600 be appropriated to provide the borough with its first hook and ladder truck, the price to be $525 F.O.B. by steamer to Bridgeport, $15 for freight to Newtown, and $60 for a shelter for the truck.

"The Budd House"
50 Main Street

Although this house, Newtown's only residential listing in the National Register of Historic Places, has generally been called "the Budd House," it was originally and officially titled "the Glover House."

Built in 1869 for Henry Beers Glover, the house has a large three-story central block with a two-story service wing to the rear. The mansard roof is covered with slate, while the house's exterior brick sidewalls are sheathed with clapboards.

One of the town's largest homes when it was constructed, the residence would have taken several servants to maintain. It is thought that there were two live-in servants, perhaps a cook-general and a parlor maid. Certainly day help, such as a charwoman and a laundress, were also employed. Several men were hired to maintain the grounds.

Mr. Glover was born in Newtown in 1824. He moved to Cleveland as a young man and returned to his hometown in the 1850s. In 1855, he joined with several other businessmen to found the Newtown Savings Bank.

When Henry Beers Glover and his wife died in the 1870s, the house became the property of their daughter Mary, wife of Yale graduate and local lawyer William Beecher. It was William and Mary's daughter Florence who provided the house with its more familiar name when she married Stephen E. Budd about 1918. After Mr. Budd died, Florence continued to live in the house until her death in 1977.

William and Carolyn Greene bought the property in 1986.

—Laura Lerman

photograph by Ken Kast

Broken Notes from a Gray Nunnery
by Julia Sherman Hallock

I have been thinking, too, of that blessed day which brought me a letter from Phyllis. I was lingering in the city, amid uncongenial surroundings, and although my work from its sheer wearisomeness brought soundest sleep at night and left little scope for sentiment by day, I was continually dreaming of the country, with a deep and homesick longing to go back and live once more among my native rocks. Phyllis had always lived among them, but she was now living absolutely alone, except for Dandy Jim, her pet cat, and her letter said, "Come!" At that word the fetters seemed to drop from my soul, and I turned my face homeward with the heart of a pilgrim, whose shrine and Mecca are in the past.

I like to recall the stormy winter day, fast waning, when, after a slow drive from the station, I reached the home end of the long lane that turns in from the narrow street, and was set down by the wide stone steps leading toward the steep yard in front of the gray old house.

Phyllis stood in the open doorway, the radiance of her self-forgetful welcome made so pathetic by the deep mourning dress she wore and the traces of grief in her face, that for a remorseful moment I was quite ashamed to have been so glad in my eagerness to fill a vacancy lately made by death.

But when after our long evening talk I retired to my pleasant south chamber, and sank into the downy deeps of an old fashioned bed, I thought I had never before known genuine repose. How still the rooms were! How wide and free the storm-swept waste outside! All night, at intervals, the wind, like a friendly watchman, came down from the cedar-sentinelled hills to gently shake the doors and windows and steal away with a long-drawn "all's well!" soothing as any cradle-song to drowsy ears. The town I had left seemed thousands of miles away.

—High Rock Road, Sandy Hook, 1896

In 1859, town Selectmen approved the building of a "pest house" in the Hattertown area to ward off one of the greatest calamities that could strike a town. The term "pest house" is derived from the word pestilence and referred to a building where victims of a deadly epidemic disease could be isolated.

In the latter years of the 1850s smallpox threatened. The outbreak can be traced to a settlement of five or six families living in the Hattertown district. Their farms were located along a road which ran from the junction of the Hattertown and Mt. Nebo roads. One of these neighbors brought the disease from New York, and the entire community subsequently was wiped out by it.

As contagion spread, a black man named Purdy who had already been struck with smallpox volunteered to take care of the afflicted. Tradition holds that he was operating a station on the "underground" and was smuggling runaway slaves into Canada. With another volunteer, name unknown, Purdy ministered to the sick and dying.

Coffins were made by one of the Parmalees who would bring the coffins as far as Mt. Nebo Road, where Purdy picked them up and probably himself dug the graves in the cemetery on the Redding border. This section of Newtown has since been known locally as Purdy Station, and a street sign so designated was later placed at the start of the abandoned road.

Education: the Districts' Influence Continues

After 40 years of control by the Newtown School Society, the different school districts were granted in 1839 powers to elect their own officers and to levy education taxes in their areas. For three-quarters of a century this method prevailed.

Each district in the town became to a large extent self-contained, like a collection of separate villages. Many had their own church, a mill or factory, and a store or two, as well as a school. The districts continued to set their own courses of study, and although there was a central Board of School Visitors, its recommendations were not always followed.

In 1842, teacher Polly Beers was paid $1.50 per week. In 1846, North Center School hired Hannah Fairchild at the sum of $2.50 per week — but she had to pay her own board. Supplying teachers was a problem. Often the winter term was taught by a farmer with little education, and the summer session might be in the hands of a very young girl who could claim only a district school training.

Dissatisfaction with many of the district schools caused private institutions to be organized in several parts of town. Taunton, Main Street, and Sandy Hook had such schools which survived for varying lengths of time.

The founding of the Newtown Academy in 1837 was brought about by the conviction that education should go beyond the district school level. Money was privately subscribed and the Academy was built on the later site of the Newtown Savings Bank. It was immediately popular and flourished with varying success and in several different buildings until 1902.

Although most of Newtown's separate school districts had been established in the 18th century, the increase in school population in Sandy Hook made one final district necessary. Walnut Tree Hill district was founded in 1886 as a result of the influx of workers employed by the New York Belting and Packing Company on the Pootatuck River.

Broken Notes from a Gray Nunnery
by Julia Sherman Hallock

We are quite cut off from communication with our kind, and know the full meaning of "twelve miles from a lemon," for the grocer's clerk does not come; we are out of kerosene and have no candles. This afternoon Phyllis has improvised a "poverty lamp" that we view with some lugubrious mirth. A sauce-plate filled with cottolene, in which a shoestring is disposed, with its two ends hanging out to await the inspiration of a match. As a burlesque on the little antique Roman lamp, it is an undoubted success. Phyllis suggests that we set it under the kitchen glass to burn before vanity's shrine; as women generally are supposed to worship there.

—High Rock Road, Sandy Hook, 1896

Religion: Workers Bring their Faith to Newtown

The new diversity of settlement in Newtown resulted in a wider ethnic base for the town's religious institutions. Some new residents were assimilated into the old established congregations; others organized to build churches affiliated with denominations never before represented in town.

Methodist meetings were held as early as 1800 in a private home near where Trinity Church was later built. They were conducted by two instructors, Joseph Pierce and Levi Buson. For a long time the members had been ministered to by circuit preachers, the nearest church being in Easton. By 1831 the first meeting house was built on Main Street, just south of the library. Soon the increasing population in Sandy Hook prompted a demand for a church located nearer the parishioners' homes, and the present church was built there in 1850.

The followers of the Universalist denomination built a large church in 1835 on Main Street, at the present site of the town hall. The membership appears to have lessened rapidly, because in 1858 the building was sold to St. Rose Parish and used for Roman Catholic services. In 1883, the building changed hands again. It became the town hall and served that purpose until the Edmond Town Hall was erected in 1929.

The first Baptist Church had been established in the 18th century at Zoar Corners. There in 1794, the Society had erected a large barn-like structure, not at all like a church. How long services were held is not known, but tradition suggests that the building was torn down in the 19th century and the timbers found their way into various barns in the neighborhood. In 1850 a smaller, well built, and well furnished edifice was erected just next to the Zoar Cemetery, and the Berkshire Pond was used for baptisms. But slowly the congregation dwindled and, after several years of disuse, the church and contents were sold at auction in 1913.

In 1831 the Zoar section of town was a populous center with mills, small shops, and factories that made up a lively community. On the hill opposite the old Gray's Plain Schoolhouse, a new house of worship was erected. This was the Episcopal Church of St. James, an offshoot of Trinity Parish. [The novel, *Shiloh*, by W. M. L. Jay, is based on life in the district of Zoar at the period, and it describes St. James Church in detail.]

The first rector had resigned from Trinity after an incumbency of 30 years, but stayed with the new parish only a very short while. St. James Parish returned to its parent. The church building was finally torn down in the 1870s and its cornerstone was set into the lawn of Trinity Church — "St. James Ch. 1831."

The potato famine in Ireland in 1840 had a direct bearing on the development of Newtown. It was just then that industrial expansion was occurring in Sandy Hook, and a large influx of Irish workers came there, ready to settle down and become a part of the new village.

There are two traditions regarding the first service held for the Roman Catholics of Newtown. The first holds that mass was celebrated in 1841 by the Reverend James Smythe, one of the pioneers of the Diocese. The second tradition estimates a date six years later when mass was celebrated in 1847 by the Reverend John Brady from Hartford at the home of Peter Leavy. There were 12 persons present at the mass. The tax list of that year contained the names of three Irish families, which could alone have made up the congregation. There was no record of Catholics living in town before 1845.

By 1858, the number of Roman Catholics had increased rapidly, and when the Reverend John Smith of Danbury purchased the Universalist Meeting House for a church, the congregation had grown to 100 members. Until this time, Newtown Catholics had been under the jurisdiction of St. Peter's Church in Danbury, which would send a priest at intervals to celebrate mass and administer the sacraments. Many of the pioneer Catholics related tales of walking to Danbury for mass when the priest could not come to Newtown.

In 1859, the first resident priest, Dr. Francis Lenihan, organized the present parish under the patronage of St. Rose of Lima. He also purchased land for the cemetery, but it was not consecrated until 1865. It contains a stone erected to the memory of Mary Cain (Keane) dated September 7, 1860, which is marked as the first burial in the cemetery.

At one time in the 1860s, New Milford was a mission of St. Rose, attended by priests from Newtown. Other parishes which they served were Oxford, Brookfield, and Southbury.

Father James McCartan came here in 1873. In order to accommodate the large portion of his congregation which lived in Sandy Hook and adjacent districts, the location of the church was transferred from Main Street to Church Hill Road. A new building was completed in 1883. Father McCartan also saw to the building of St. Patrick's Hall behind the church and a rectory on the west side of the grounds. When a newer rectory was built in 1895 on the east side of the church, the older one became a convent.

St. Stephen's Church in Stepney continued to operate as a mission of St. Rose until 1934. A parochial school in Sandy Hook was built by the incumbent priest, Father Fox, in 1896 and prospered until the closing of the New York Belting and Packing

Company in 1900. At that time, many families left town with the factory and the school was closed.

St. John's Episcopal Church in Sandy Hook was established as an off-spring of Trinity Parish. The first building was erected in 1868 under the conditions of a bequest of William B. Glover. It was then a diocesan mission. The parish of St. John's was organized in 1880, and the Guild, which came into being at the same time, became an important factor in the support of the church. In 1929, the original structure burned to the ground, but five years later a new building was completed. The present church was consecrated in 1934.

The town's youngest church of the 19th century seems to have died in infancy. We know that a Union Chapel was erected in Taunton district in 1878, but beyond that fact the records are silent.

The Economy: Farm and Factory

The industrial revolution profoundly altered (and sometimes overwhelmed) cities and towns all over America. Newtown experienced the prosperity brought by an expanding economy, but the town was to remain, throughout the 19th century, primarily a rural and agricultural community.

As Newtown entered the 1800s, farming was unchallenged as the major profession. Livestock continued as an economic staple. Although there is no record of the number of sheep in the town before 1800, references show that an important factor in the farmer's economy continued to be his flock. Each man at this time was allowed 30 head of the town flock. Each year a sheep master was appointed and he hired a shepherd, who was employed at $12 per month, "if not to be had for a lower price." For many years, the shepherd was assisted by a worker named Caesar, one of Newtown's small number of black residents.

The season for the common flock began in early June (after the sheep had been sheared and when the new lambs were old enough to be turned loose) and lasted until late September. The sheep master collected the sheep from the different school districts, planned the route or "drift" to be followed during the summer, chose the best common land for pasturage, and arranged for overnight "yarding" in safely enclosed fields.

In 1823 the Newtown Sheep Company was formed. Moss K. Botsford was chosen sheep master for that year. The route for collecting the flock was as follows:

Long time resident of Newtown, Marguerite Raynolds, tells a story about a farmer who would herd his turkeys to market in Bridgeport every year: "He always started very early in the morning down Route 25, that, did you know, used to be an old Indian trail? Turkeys always roost at night, so when darkness came, his turkeys would just settle themselves up all snug in the trees and the farmer'd go home for his supper and a good night's sleep. Next morning he'd arrive back where he left his flock just before sun up, and it would only be a matter of a few minutes before all those old birds would be on the way again."

—Newtown Legend as told to Linda Napier

. . .from Chestnut Tree Hill through Zoar to Ebenezer Beers, thence through Toddy Hill to Caesar's, . . . thence through Taunton, Palestine, Land's End and Hanover to Wapping, and thence through Sandy Hook to Newtown Street.

This drive was expected to be accomplished in about eight days. When the entire flock was collected, the shepherd and a boy hired for $3 or $4 a month to help him, started on the season's tour. The shepherd and the boy would start with nearly 1,000 sheep toward the first night's stopping place, about a "ten-hour feeding drift" away. At night, with the sheep enclosed in a farmer's field, the shepherd and the boy were provided with their "keep" and a night's rest.

All through the summer the flock moved along the pre-arranged route until the sheep master ordered disbanding in September. The final round-up was held at Caleb Baldwin's on Newtown Street (the second house south of Trinity Church). Here the owners gathered for the breaking up of the flock and to claim their own sheep.

The sheep business was profitable until about 1860 when the establishment of the Beecher Satinet Factory in Sandy Hook sharply cut the local demand for wool.

As in the early days of the town's history, roads and bridges were of great importance to the economy at the beginning of the new century.

In 1797, Christopher Colles published the first map of Main Street which indicated that it was part of the old Military Road from Stratford to Poughkeepsie. In Newtown, a blacksmith shop and tavern were located on the dirt road in the center of town. The northwest extension was a twisting, climbing cart path crossing back and forth over Route 6 (then Slut's Hill).

At the turn of the century, towns had not kept up their roads and the state provided no monies for this purpose. Thus turnpikes came into use.

Newtown and its neighboring towns fought over the establishment of a Turnpike Corporation. The proposed corporation would build and maintain a toll road from New Milford to the city line of Bridgeport.

Although other towns along the route favored it enthusiastically, Newtown was opposed to the venture.

In 1800, Newtown protested to the general assembly against the granting of a charter and objected to having "our road obstructed by turnpikes and gates." The assembly did not act. By the next session in 1801 a change of feeling had come over

photograph by William R. Greene

The Ram Pasture, South Main Street.

Newtown's 2,903 inhabitants, and it was voted not to oppose the turnpike. Therefore, the assembly granted a charter to the Bridgeport and Newtown Turnpike Corporation permitting the erection of three toll gates.

No tolls were charged for travelers on their way to church, to funerals or to the grist mills. Four-wheeled pleasure carriages with driver and passenger paid 25¢; a rider on horseback, 4¢; sleighs with two horses and driver, 8¢; stage coaches, 25¢; horses, mules, and cattle, 1¢ each. In 1839 the rates were raised on pleasure carriages "hung on springs of steel, leather or iron."

In spite of local misgivings , Newtown profited greatly by the turnpike. The town became the midway stopping point for man and beast. A round trip for ox-drawn carts loaded with produce or other goods took three days from New Milford to Bridgeport, and Newtown caught them coming and going. Inns and taverns profited from the traffic, especially from the stage coaches.

By 1829, the stages were running on regular routes and almost regular schedules. Horses were changed in Newtown, and the passengers required food or lodging before starting off again on trips to Hartford, Bridgeport, Norwalk, Litchfield, "Sing Sing," or New York.

The Newtown Turnpike roughly followed Main Street from the Monroe town line to the present monument, proceeded up Currituck Road to Whisconier Hill, and into New Milford at Gallows Hill. Its southern end was at the north line of the newly incorporated borough called Bridgeport.

The turnpike was narrow, only 12 feet wide at the town line, 14 feet at the Pootatuck River, 18 feet by the Ram Pasture, and 24 feet wide ascending the hill into the borough. There were two toll gates in Newtown: the North Gate in Hawleyville, about a mile south of the Brookfield line, and the Middle Gate on the Monroe town line.

The Bridgeport-Newtown Turnpike was later joined by one from Bennett's Bridge to Westport (the Monroe-Newtown Turnpike) which followed present day Hattertown Road, and many other toll roads. The Bridgeport-Newtown Turnpike Corporation was in operation for almost 90 years. Many of the others failed to survive as financial enterprises.

By 1870, the condition of the roads throughout Newtown was a subject for bitter complaint. The highway from Sandy Hook to Newtown was an unsatisfactory one, especially on the steep grade of Church Hill as it rose to Newtown (Main) Street.

Boggy roads were particularly trying, and one of the methods used to improve them was "blotting" — dumping cartloads of sawdust on wet stretches. As far back as 1885, there was agitation to build a sidewalk from Sandy Hook to Newtown, to cost not more than $2,000. The sidewalk was not built.

Transport by or across Newtown's waterways was also a subject for much discussion in the 19th century. Early on, the rivers, with their seasonal fluctuations, nearly always prevailed over attempts to develop permanent crossings.

In 1801 Hanover Road was known as Hawley's Bridge Road, but later maps show the road terminating at Hanover ford, mute testimony that the river had here resisted an attempted bridge.

A town meeting was held in April of 1822. Mindful of Newtown's need to transport its products to markets, it was "voted to incorporate a company for the purpose of establishing navigation on the Housatonic River by means of a canal near its bank or by improving the bed of the river as far as the state line." Other towns were not in favor of such a canal so the project was never started.

By 1850, two bridges (both toll) served Newtown. Bennett's Bridge connected the Zoar and Wapping districts of Sandy Hook to the Kettletown district of Southbury.

Illustration from *Broken Notes from a Gray Nunnery* (1896) by Julia Sherman Hallock.

Zoar Bridge connected the Halfway River district of Sandy Hook and the Monroe Turnpike in Monroe with the town of Oxford and the Derby Turnpike.

The last Zoar toll bridge, later replaced by the Stevenson Dam road, was a wooden frame, steel cable suspension bridge. In spring thaws, the ice would break and pile up under the bridge, but its novel construction allowed this bridge to "ride the ice" downstream and settle back in pendulum fashion when the ice thawed. By this means, the Zoar toll bridge survived for many years on a site that had destroyed its predecessors.

One drawback of the unusual construction was that the narrow one-lane bridge would sway in a brisk wind. Horses seemed to adapt well to the swaying but an ox team was a comical sight as nigh ox (the lead ox on the driver's left) and off ox (the lead ox on the driver's right) leaned into each other to counter this unexpected motion under their feet.

Roads, rivers, and, eventually, rails all contributed to the need for further accommodation and entertainment in the town. In the 1800s, several new inns were established.

Dr. Gideon Shepherd's Inn stood on the corner of Church Hill Road and The Boulevard. It was a rendezvous for sleighing parties and other local gaieties. The sign swaying from the post in front read "A plain Tavern for plain folks, kept by a plain man" and on the reverse was the suggestion "if not suited, the road opens both ways." Since this inn was on the stage route to Hartford, it was well patronized.

Continuing down the hill on this east to west stage route was the Sandy Hook Hotel, which was for a considerable time under the management of B. Gregory. This hostelry also served north bound New Haven to Hartford stage travelers.

About 1820 Sallu Pell Barnum started another roadside tavern in a house where the Cyrenius H. Booth Library was later built. This was eventually acquired by W. H. Dick, and in the 1880s was flourishing as Dick's Hotel. It burned down in 1897 and the Newtown Inn (erected on its site) became a very popular hotel for summer boarders.

Also doing a thriving business in the 1880s was Brown's Hotel, run by George H. Brown, proprietor, and F. R. M. Chapman, manager. This establishment was known later as the Grand Central Hotel, then as the Parker House, and finally as the Yankee Drover Inn.

One more inn on the turnpike was the Middlebrook. Situated almost on the Monroe line, this establishment was not much of a factor in Newtown life, but it was popular with travelers on the late stage from Bridgeport.

To supply farms and households in the 19th century, business and commerce were growing.

There were two general stores. The Brick Store was founded on its Sandy Hook site in 1831. The Newtown General Store on Main Street opened during the Civil War.

In 1855, the Newtown Savings Bank was organized under the leadership of Henry Beers Glover. This local business institution has boasted a lengthy career and celebrated its 100th anniversary in 1955.

The Newtown Bee was started in 1877 by John T. Pearse of Bethel, with the financial backing of A. A. Bensel. Pearse, a reportedly gifted but eccentric character, developed a weekly newspaper on an unreliable schedule that assured eventual failure.

In 1880, the *Bee* was purchased and revitalized by Reuben Henry Smith. *The Chronicle*, a rival local paper published by a Mr. Madigan, was bought out by the Smith family, and *The Newtown Bee* moved to larger quarters on Main Street in 1882.

Ten years later, Reuben Smith retired, and the business was taken over by his brothers Allison B. and Arthur J. They provided the same vigorous and involved leadership that was to keep the *Bee* at the forefront of Newtown's commercial endeavors in the 20th century.

When industry came to the community, it changed the face of Sandy Hook. The Pootatuck River made this area an ideal location for factories.

Around 1820, Barber's History refers to "the flourishing village of Sandy Hook" with the "fine mill stream (the Pootatuck) running northerly at the foot of an almost perpendicular bluff 160 ft. high."

The financial crash of 1837 had an adverse effect upon these factories and on some of the local home industries. However, the businesses as a whole were built on sound financial structures and weathered the storm.

An astonishingly varied list of products was being made in Sandy Hook, Zoar and nearby centers, and, to a smaller extent, in Newtown at this time. There were many small plants manufacturing horn combs and buttons, importing "horns and hooves from Buenos Aires," as well as metal-casting shops for brass keys, reinforced pewter spoons, and parts for shotguns and files. In the woodworking trades, furniture, wooden screws, sleighs, carriages, and coffins all were turned out to meet the demands of the expanding nation. The New York Belting and Packing Company, "the largest institution of its kind in the world," made a tremendous impact on the town economy.

Newtown's connection with the rubber industry began in the 1830s. Charles Goodyear was born in New Haven, and his sister married a Sandy Hook resident. Young Goodyear spent many hours experimenting with rubber in his brother-in-law's factory in the Glen. He discovered the process of the vulcanization of rubber in 1839, and the commercial possibilities of the new material were quickly realized by enterprising manufacturers. Goodyear himself never became wealthy from his inventions.

In 1845, Samuel Curtis founded S. Curtis & Son, Inc. in the Berkshire section of Sandy Hook. The factory manufactured combs and buttons, and later converted to the production of folding paper boxes.

Industrial ventures also reflected interest in the mineral deposits of the town. Several mines were opened. One of the first was mentioned in Charles Burr Todd's *In Old Connecticut*:

> *Lower down the Housatonic Valley at Sandy Hook in Newtown, we have a gold mine which was worked by British Soldiers in the Revolution and casks of its ore were sent to England for treatment. From one pound of its ore 75 cents in gold and 11 cents in silver were taken, if the assayer is to be believed.*

An attempt to obtain coal was also made in Sandy Hook on the banks of the Pootatuck River. Samples proved to contain very little carbon, however, and plans for further excavations were abandoned.

Near the coal mine site another mine was mentioned in Charles Upham Shepard's "A Report on the Geological Survey of Connecticut," dated 1837:

> At Sandy Hook, Newtown, about 50 rods north of the spot where search was made for coal, is a tunnel carried for a short distance through a projecting quartz vein contained in mica-slate. It is called a silvermine. Attached to the walls of this excavation, traces of galena and iron pyrite were observable.

Dr. Shepard also mentioned Judson's quarry at the corner of Rock Ridge Road and Birch Hill Road, which was once an important source of gneissoid flagging stone.

Captain Cook's Quarry, once a mica surface mine, was located at the end of Purdy Station Road. This interesting site also offers views of surrounding hillsides and white rock formations. It has been cited in a state publication as being of "State significance."

Perhaps less exciting but by far the most economically significant mining in Newtown was found in deposits of sand and gravel in the Pootatuck River Valley. These were left behind by the large volumes of meltwater carrying debris out from the front of the melting glacier.

By 1835, Newtown and all the Housatonic Valley towns realized that transportation facilities must be developed in order to reach markets. The more venturesome advocated construction of a railroad to connect Bridgeport with the distant trade center of Albany, and from there to the limitless west. Shares were sold, money flowed in, and the start was made at Bridgeport three years later.

All work was done by hand or with one-horse dumpcarts. When the crews reached Newtown and made the tunnel at Hawleyville, it was the wonder of the countryside. The railroad, third of its kind in the state, was constructed very quickly. The first passenger train made the trip from New Milford to Bridgeport on February 14, 1840.

In 1872 the New York, New Haven and Hartford Railroad was formed. Over a period of years the consolidated company acquired most of the small New England lines. In 1892 the Housatonic became the Berkshire Division of the New Haven. Later the Shepaug became the Litchfield Division of the the New York, and the New

Right, excerpts from "Earcuts of Creatures." Record Book courtesy of Town Clerk's Office.

1819

William Baldwin his ear mark

Ezekiel Beers his ear mark

Philo Beers his ear mark

Henry Beers his ear mark

Caleb Baldwin Town Clerk

59

England became the Highland Division.

The trains made stops in Botsford, Newtown, North Newtown, Hanover Springs, and Hawleyville. The first person in town to buy stock in the Housatonic Railroad was Daniel Botsford, a wealthy man who at one time owned more land than anyone else in Newtown. His son Jabez served as station agent for many years.

Townspeople began to commute to businesses in other areas. By 1853, stage-coaches made connections at Newtown station for towns not served by the railroad, and the traffic rapidly increased.

Trains were not universally popular. Some towns did not permit them to run on Sunday and others restricted their passage until after the hours of church services. The July of 1853 issue of the "Academician" (published by the pupils of the Newtown Academy) reported an accident to the Reverend Mr. O. H. Smith of Redding Ridge. When his horse was frightened by the train, and his carriage was over-turned, Mr. Smith complained that "the engineer, although he saw the whole occurrence, passed on without stopping to render any assistance. Are such men fit to be engineers?"

As more powerful coal burning engines became available to navigate steeper slopes along the Housatonic River, the Housatonic Railroad entered into a joint venture with the New Haven and Derby Railroad and opened Derby Extension in 1888.

In 1881, Hawleyville is described as a great railroad center. "The Housatonic Road from Bridgeport to Pittsfield and on to the state line, the New York and New England Road from Brewster's Station on the Harlem Road to everywhere down east, the Shepaug Road from Danbury, its hats and its Danbury-News-Man, to Litchfield, crossed each other here."

A train trip of the day would "pass through the little stations and quiet hamlets of Stepney and Botsford, and press on till we reach the pleasant region of Newtown, so pleasant indeed that during the summer months its homes are well filled, its road-ways thronged and its broad acres rambled over by numberless guests from the cities, who get good air, good living, rest and recreation, health and strength at very reasonable rates, as far as dollars and cents are concerned."

—Revision by Mary Jane (Bunny) Madden
of material from *Newtown: Past and Present*, 1975

Map of the Pootatuck River and its two
source-branches. Courtesy of Al Goodrich

An Industrial Evolution: The Pootatuck's Progress through Newtown History

The Pootatuck is Newtown's most historic and unfailing resource. Its role in the town economy serves as an indicator of industrial highs and lows and of the changing character of the area's population

This small waterway springs from two sources: North Branch from a swamp near the intersection of Route 302 and Key Rock Road, and South Branch from Guskie's pond situated at 500 feet above sea-level over the Newtown border into Monroe. Drawing from a watershed of 26.1 miles, passing through swamps and ravines lined with hemlock and oak, then quiet, sun-drenched meadows, the two branches meet in a grassy field south of Resurrection Cemetery west of Route 25.

Meandering through gradually descending grades, the Pootatuck's speed escalates south of Sandy Hook, and, once in the gorge near Church Hill Road bridge, it foams over boulders and rocks in turbulent rapids. As the streambed widens and reaches the lower part of Glen Road, water pours over two dams once used to power major factories. Sometimes, after severe rain, it flings itself forty feet out beyond the dam to crash down over rocky bottoms. Then finally, 9.1 miles from Guskie Pond, it flows peacefully into Lake Zoar and loses its ancient identity in the Housatonic River.

Centuries back, the Pootatuck supported Indians of that name occupying the regions along the Housatonic. When the colonists arrived in the early 1700s, the river provided water-power for gristmills and sawmills. Then, when the pastoral interlude of the agricultural era gave way to the dynamic 1840s, the river came into its inexhaustible, productive own. The Pootatuck with its mills and factories, large and small, converted Sandy Hook from a placid village into a humming and populous industrial center.

Two events were catalytic. Born in 1800 in New Haven, Charles Goodyear came to live in Sandy Hook with his sister, Mrs. Josiah Tomlinson. Poor and so thin that the locals called him a scarecrow, Goodyear set up a small laboratory where the lower factory would later stand. There, he accidentally discovered how to vulcanize rubber. While making chemical experiments with crude rubber mixed with sulphur, he dropped some of the mix on a hot stove. Earlier efforts had been unable to tolerate both heat and cold; this rubber substance withstood the heat and became elastic and strong. Eventually, the commercial use of rubber became possible.

The second event so crucial to the Pootatuck's success occurred in 1840 and 1841 when local carpenters laid a railroad bed through Newtown so that the Housatonic Railroad could run from Bridgeport through Monroe and Newtown to Pittsfield, Massachusetts. The most important stop was Hawleyville, where the Housatonic line could connect with rails from Danbury, Norwalk and Fishkill, N. Y. The connection tied two small isolated communities (Newtown Borough and the Pootatuck`area) to the world of trade already running in high gear along the eastern seaboard.

The first factories to capitalize on the new transportation resource were located upstream near Cold Spring Road, their machinery powered by waterwheel. Buying carload lots of horn and hoof from the stockyards of Buffalo, Kansas City, Chicago, and South Omaha, they quickly learned how to clarify, cut, and press the raw materials into buttons for the clothing and underwear trades. In addition they made ladies' combs, then in high fashion, in all shapes and sizes.

In the Berkshire section of Sandy Hook, a fast-flowing tributary to the Pootatuck provided power near its confluence with the river where S. Curtis & Son built a factory manufacturing more buttons and combs in 1845. Implicit in the wording of the lease was a euphoria about the future of this business that was typical of the period: "It will run to the end of time."

The Niantic, or so-called "Shoddy" Mill, came

Bridge and rapids at the intersection of Church Hill Road and Route 34 in Sandy Hook.

Photograph by Mary Mitchell

next, a three story factory with a tenement-office and storehouse on a two-acre lot near Route 25 in Botsford. Powered by an overshot water-wheel 45 feet in diameter, the mill made satinet, a kind of cloth of cotton warp and woolen filling used to make trousers, ladies' dress goods and horse blankets.

Outpacing these smaller operations was a large brick mill erected in 1846 in the modish Italianate style by the New York Belting and Packaging Company. (Later called the Rocky

Glen Mill, its original brick shell was retained and converted in the 1980s into an office building.)

With a work force of 250 hands, the mill shipped elevator belts, rubber mailbags, and other applications of the Goodyear patents to sites as far away as Texas. Mostly sons of Erin fleeing the Irish potato famine, the employees soon nestled into Walnut Tree Hill (or Mount Pisgah, as the Indians called it), brought over their relatives, and stirred up the local economic,

religious, and political scene.

In 1914, a reporter from *The Newtown Bee* persuaded a Mr. Patch, eighty-three years old, to reminisce about the 1850s. "We had a plastermill, carriage manufactury at the sawmill, dressmakers, tailors and custom boot-makers, iron and brass founders. The gristmill built by Samuel Sanford in 1712 was still grinding grain. Rivets and wooden screws were being made in the Dutch rubber factory (known also as the upper factory)."

By the early 1900s though, electricity began to replace water power and turn turbines instead of wheels. The biggest employer, the New York Belting and Packing Company, moved to Passaic,

62

Photograph by Al Goodrich
Confluence of Pootatuck and Housatonic Rivers at the north end of Glen Road.

New Jersey. A grave conflict faced the crowded but entrenched Irish community. Should families separate, some moving to Passaic, others remaining in Sandy Hook to see what would happen? Should the young skilled worker with a fiancée employed at a button shop try his wings in the wider world and later send for her? Many families did uproot and move away, while others decided to try their Irish luck and stay.

And the luck did hold. The Fabric Fire Hose Company soon moved into the lower factory, opening up 200 jobs. The Premier Manufacturing Company hitherto housed in Berkshire, moved its machinery into the upper factory to manufacture products such as drills, lathes, and presses,

Photograph by Mary Mitchell
Flood gate control at lower factory.

63

based on the newly-invented electric airpump. The decision of this firm to increase its capital stock to $1,000,000 in 1923 echoes the overall national prosperity of the post-World War I era. Still other jobs opened up when the innovative Niantic Mill retooled to print sets of Dickens, Trollope, and other popular English authors. Manufacturing army blankets and cutting furs for a Danbury company, then later adapting again to enter the bakelite market, the mill was so successful that it had to put on a night shift in 1931.

Fortunes, however, turned again, as they have a way of doing. With the Depression, residents of the Big Apple searching for less stressful life-styles found Newtown with its relatively inexpensive, well-built old houses, high and picturesque on wooded hills and convenient to commuters on the old Housatonic, now the New York, New Haven & Hartford Railroad. Factory employment along the Pootatuck slackened, its industry faded out, and its posture fell to a low ebb. A new era of residential and recreational usage began for the little river.

Contemporary road maps reflected the change. From having seen their name printed in large letters, Sandy Hookers now endured the ignominy of small print — second place to quiet, residential Newtown. The Pootatuck, however, long referred to as the Brook in old deeds and documents, was now designated a river. Permanent and vacation homes along this stretch of water became premium locations for settling during the 20th Century. Despite occasional struggles with flood waters, residents and passers-by valued the beauty of the Pootatuck — quiet once again.

—Mary Mitchell

Family Life in the 19th Century: The Home Perspective on History

Newtown had a chiefly agrarian economy, and life centered around the family farm throughout the 19th century. Even the town's doctors, lawyers, bankers, and new breed of industrialists engaged in farming to supply the needs of their families.

The town was also a popular resort during this period. The fresh mountain air, pure spring water, and abundant lakes and ponds attracted people who were able to travel here via four major railroads in addition to horse and carriage.

This was the eve of the major innovations: electricity, telephones, automobiles, and advances in medicine and technology which would drastically and irrevocably change the way people lived. People were much more self-sufficient then than now, providing their own food, building their own homes and barns, and making most of their own clothes and household implements, with the help of friends and family.

Some long deceased residents, through their writing or oral histories, provide us a window into what home life was like.

A Journal of Newtown
March 29, 1831 - November 18, 1832
by Beach Camp

A descendent of some of Newtown's original settlers, Beach Camp was an active participant in the affairs of the town and in Trinity Church. At the time he wrote his journal, he was a new husband and very proud of it, according to entries he made.

"Six months this day I was joined to Catharine in wedlock by Rev. Daniel Burhans," he wrote on April 27, 1831. Throughout the rest of the journal he consistently called her "wife." Her maiden

Iron bicycle from the early 1800s, in the historical collection, Cyrenius H. Booth Library.

Photograph by Joseph I. Kugielsky

65

name was Catharine M. Foot.

In June he noted, "Eight months this day since I became a husband." In commemoration of his first anniversary he wrote: "The first anniversary of our marriage celebrated by me in shop and by wife at home making applesauce."

The Camps moved to a small farm on Mt. Pleasant Road. during the course of the journal. Their house, located just past the junction of Routes 25 and 6, was later occupied by the Mt. Pleasant Hospital for Animals.

Mr. Camp was among a group of enterprising farmers who were also involved in the manufacture of items to bring to market in the cities of Bridgeport, Norwalk, and New York. He had a shop in which he made horn combs in what seemed, even to his 19th century sensibility, a laborious fashion.

"Comb making dull in the extreme," he noted April, 16, 1831.

Attending church services on the Sabbath figured prominently in the life of the Camps as for other Newtown families of various denominations and faiths. During mild weather, they would walk the three hilly miles from their home on Mt. Pleasant Road to Trinity Church.

"Clark, Sarah Ann, Wife and myself walk to church. Had a passage home. No priest," he

photograph courtesy Jim Gunn

wrote May 22, 1831. The church was without a priest during the first few months that he kept his journal. Rather than listening to an uninspiring sermon delivered by a lay person, the Camps would often travel to Danbury or Brookfield, a considerable journey.

"Harnessed two horses forward of the wagon and went in it to Danbury to church," he wrote on June 12, 1831.

"This is a remarkable day for this town; not a clergyman of any denomination officiates in this town. Mr. Stratten, who has been hired by the Episcopal Society and was expected here today, has been detained by sickness in his family," was his entry for September 25, 1831.

" . . . Singing is in a low state at present," Mr. Camp commented December 11, 1831. Not one to make idle complaints, he promptly took the personal initiative to improve the vocal arts at Trinity Church.

"Held a singing school at Mr. Stratten's house. Had nineteen scholars," he recorded February 18, 1832. "Held a school for the instruction of young singers at Charles Clark's," was his entry for March 3, 1832. He subsequently held singing schools at the homes of each of the parishioners for the instruction of their children.

Mr. Camp frequently commented on the quality of sermons and quoted Bible verses which were part of the Sunday services. His religious convictions carried over into his daily life, including the hope for a bountiful farming season and his response to the birth of his first child.

"Farmers commence the cultivation of the earth. May it please the Lord to bless our labors for our good here and hereafter," he wrote April 8, 1831.

"Wife put to bed with her first born child - a fine boy, weighing nine and one half pounds.

Mother and child comfortable. A parent's care and anxiety now commences and sometimes perhaps there is greater cause to weep at one's birth than at one's death. Man seems to be born to trouble, but death frees him from it if a life of piety and devotion be led," was his entry of May 23, 1832.

The news of the birth of his son comes as something of a shock to the reader. Although he had been writing for 14 months, and he was clearly pleased to announce it, he made no mention of his wife's pregnancy.

Certain passages reinforce the self-sufficiency and hard work inherent in 19th century life. On August 2, 1831, he "made a butter stick—Went to the saw mill and helped measure and load 616 feet of board for Russell Lacey — Got up two loads of oats."

On August 25, 1831, he "went to mill with two bushels of rye, which makes six and one half bushels I have had ground since I moved. Bent combs. Wife done spinning."

In October of that year, he "made two pudding sticks for Wife, finished threshing buckwheat. Been a very fine week for farmers to gather in their crops." He "helped Cyrus butcher two hogs, weight 621 pounds," on December 21, 1831.

He mentioned taxes matter-of-factly on December 19, 1831: "Town meeting in the afternoon which was an adjourned town meeting, taxes laid. Town tax three cents, highway tax two cents, state tax one cent."

Death cast an ever-present shadow over people's lives. Mr. Camp recorded the passing away of numerous individuals, many of them children or young adults. Most of the deaths were attributable to diseases for which there were then no cures or treatments, such as cholera, measles, typhoid fevers, or influenza. "Lung fever," "numb palsy," and childbirth also took their toll.

His reports on the deaths of certain people are particularly touching. With tragic sadness he told of the funeral of the wife and child of the priest who had only recently assumed the helm of Trinity Church.

His entry of January 13, 1832, reads: "The funeral of the wife of Rev. S. C. Stratten was attended by a large concourse of people . . . Her infant which had been buried one week when she died was disinterred and laid in the grave beside her."

February 13, 1832 was a dark day for Newtown. "Remarkable! The bell tolled for three deaths before eleven o'clock," he wrote.

He further lamented on March 22, 1831: "Clarinda Fairchild was removed from the scene of action by death last evening, after an illness of about two weeks. A flower plucked at its opening."

His serious concern over his wife's health in December, 1831 was easily comprehensible in light of the heavy toll death exerted over young people. He recorded on December 22, 1831: "Wife taken with a severe cold - pains and aches throughout system - Tried to sweat her, but w/o effect."

The following day, she was "still worse, having a very tight hard cough, succeeded this evening in making her rest."

On December 26, 1831, "Wife remained ill. Fearful about the result..." The next day he did something 19th century farmers only considered under extreme conditions: "Called on Dr. Judson to come out to see my wife."

She recovered, and she and Mr. Camp both enjoyed a full, long life.

Diaries by Henry Beers
in five volumes
written during the 1850's and 1860's

The importance of farming to professional people is highlighted in Henry Beers' diaries. Mr. Beers was the first President of the Newtown Savings Bank, and a citizen of considerable social standing within the community. He also served as President of the Newtown Academy, a private boarding and day school. Mr. Beers was a contemporary of Beach Camp, who mentioned him a number of times in his journal with reference to borrowing a note.

Written in the precise and elegant long hand of the period, his diaries focused primarily on the everyday operations of managing his extensive farmlands and on the weather conditions which profoundly affected farming success. Every entry began with the direction of the wind, the temperature at noon and a description of the weather that day.

He had as many as six hired hands, mostly Irish immigrants, working for him on the farm at any given time. He provided detailed descriptions of the work they did, which included, among other jobs, sawing and cutting wood, carting hay, threshing rye, picking winter apples, digging stone, butchering livestock, shoveling manure, and planting.

A vestryman at Trinity Church, he quoted the scriptures read during services each Sunday and described the sermon, with commentary. He also recounted the weddings and deaths of individuals within the community that impressed him. For instance he noted February 23, 1856, "Isaac Peck, the oldest man in town died today, aged 97 years, six months."

He was an astute reader of daily newspapers, including *The New York Times*, as a passage entered in his Journal on February 8, 1861 attests: "The very coldest day. . . no cars and of course no mail today. A rare occurrence to be deprived of New York papers."

He wrote extensively of current affairs and the secessionist war which he repudiated. On December 20, 1860, he noted: "South Carolina secedes from the nation," and on March 4, 1861: "inauguration of President Lincoln today. Fine day."

1855 Sept 4th I presented my son Booth C. Beers the following
Maxims or rules for his personal government

1st Taste no intoxicating liquors, Use no tobacco
2nd Take nothing that you do not own
3rd Be attentive to business – never be idle
4th Seek no low company, Good character is inestimable
5th Be courteous to all, Politeness costs but little
6th Never put off any duty till tomorrow, that can be done to day
7th Never say I can't do any thing necessary to be done, but I will try
8th Love the truth for the truth's sake & for your own sake
9th Make no promises that you cannot perform
10th Remember "the fear of the Lord is the beginning of wisdom"
11th Take heed to do the thing that is right for that will bring
    "a man peace at the last"
12th Be modest and unassuming in your deportment
13th Think before you speak
14th Remember under all circumstances that honesty
    is the best policy
15 Keep your own secrets if you have any
16th Never play at any game of chance
17th Earn money before you spend it
18 Ever live within your income
19 Never borrow if you can possibly avoid it.
20th Never speak evil of any one

His entry of April 15, 1861 expressed the high esteem in which he held President Lincoln: "Thus it will be found at last that we have a President of firmness and substance at governing." On September 22, 1862, he announced: "This day the President issued his proclamation declaring all slaves free on the first of January next . . ."

He summed up his feelings about the war in a passage he wrote May 23, 1863: "Providence smiles upon us in the productions of the earth - while he scourges us in a rebellion, an internal domestic war, by which we are being punished for our national sins. When it will terminate, God only knows."

He also wrote of newsworthy local affairs. On June 1, 1855, he noted: "Doc Taylor taken up for attempt to commit a rape upon the daughter of William Platt and bound over in $1000 bond." On March 4, 1856, his entry read: "A. M. Foot, tavern keeper at Woodbury, was murdered and found under the shed by the Episcopal Church."

He addressed his second wife, Julia, as "Mrs. B." or "Mrs. Beers." He had been made a widower by his first wife, Betsy Glover, with whom he had no children. He called his daughter Charlotte "Lotty" and seldom mentioned his daughter Julia who presumably did not live at home when he wrote his diaries. He also had a son, Booth, who attended Newtown Academy with Lotty.

The Academy's roster of students included the surnames of many of Newtown's founding and prominent families. A school newsletter, *The Academician*, was published monthly and included information about the school and town, student essays and advertisements. Lotty and Booth were frequently contributing essayists.

He commented about the school on June 19, 1855: "The Academy closes today so far as Mr. French (the Principal) is concerned. He is under the necessity of leaving on account of misdemeanor."

The following September, "Booth becomes a clerk to Henry Sanford" and Lotty enrolled at the Sacker Institute in Brooklyn, New York, "to get an education."

On September 4, 1855, Mr. Beers presented to Booth 25 "maxims or axles for his personal government." First on the list was: "Taste no intoxicating liquors, use no tobacco." Last was: "Read over these maxims frequently and remember they are from your affectionate father, Henry Beers" [see excerpt opposite].

During the course of his journal dated April 20, 1860 - November 19, 1862, Mr. Beers provided nearly daily reports on Booth's health. His son was by this time suffering from a long, fatal illness.

In September, 1860, Booth must have been feeling better because he wrote: "Booth and I went to the county fair at Danbury this afternoon. No cattle exhibited today. Fair share of apples and other vegetables - Nothing extra." The following day father and son went to a cattle show, and the next day, Booth returned to the Fair with Lotty and some friends.

His condition worsened, and on April 2, 1861 Booth called his family to his bedside to express his dying request, which his father recorded. Booth said, "That he intended should he have lived to be a comfort to his parents and sustain them in their old age." He urged Lotty to listen to the advice and council of her parents and make her peace with God if she expected to enjoy life.

On April 14, 1861, he died at the age of 22. Mr. Beers was a religious man and, deeply aggrieved, wrote on the day of his son's funeral: "Booth Glover Beers is no more to be seen or heard on earth by us, but we feel a well grounded assurance that his soul rests in happiness and that we shall again see and know him hereafter, when our spirits shall be called away from these earthly scenes to an heavenly inheritance. We mourn, therefore, bitterly, that we shall see his face no more here forever."

Mr. and Mrs. Beers both passed away but a few years later. He died at the age of 72 on November 19, 1864. She followed him to the grave three days later at the age of 61.

"The Domestic Economy of Our Mothers" by Jane Eliza Johnson in *Newtown's History* by Ezra Levan Johnson. (pp253-259)

Jane Eliza Johnson originally presented this chapter of her husband's book at a meeting of the Pomona Grange in 1899. Born in 1837, Mrs. Johnson reflected on her own mother's housekeeping arrangements, asserting: "Nothing more fascinating to me could have been assigned as object of a paper."

She described the arduous baking process which housewives performed during the mid-19th century: "Stoves were found in most houses seventy-five years ago, but few of them had ovens that could be used for general baking: consequently every housewife heated her brick-oven twice or three times each week in summer or once or twice in winter."

She explained how, "The expression, 'have you come for fire?' is still used occasionally, but in these days when friction matches are in every home and in some pocket of almost every man, it is likely that many have no idea of the origin of the question. Every woman expected to keep coals enough buried in some fireplace to start a fire when needed. It was a sorry time when they and the tinder-box failed. My grandmother once went nearly a half-mile for coals when she lost fire.

". . .The housewife must have needed to have her wits about her to have bread, cake and pies ready to go into the oven at the same time and when the heat was just right, the bread light

Queens Cake

1 Pound of Flour 1 lb of Sugar,
3/4 lb Butter 5 Eggs 1 gill of Wine
1 of Brandy, 1 of Cream, Scald
them together when cool add
to the other ingredients 1 Nutmeg
Mrs Hopkins Recipe Oct, 1831.

Pound Cake

1 lb of Flour 1 lb of Sugar 3/4 lb
Butter and 10 Eggs

Sponge Cake

Half a Pound of Flour 1 lb of Sugar
10 Eggs and a little Salt

Wedding Cake

1 Pound of Flour 1 lb of Sugar
1 lb of Butter 10 Eggs Add Raisins
Currants and whatever Spices
you please. Ice it over with
whites of Eggs and loaf Sugar and
a little essence of Lemon well
beat together. 1816

Composition Cake

14 Ounces of Flour 10 Ounces of
Sugar 6 Ounces of Butter 2 Eggs
half a teaspoonful Pearlash half
pint of milk 1 Glass of Wine
Nutmeg and other spices

Desserts from the 19th century cookbook of Sarah Booth, grandmother of Mary Elizabeth Hawley.
Courtesy of The Cyrenius H. Booth Library Collection.

enough, yet not too light; the cake mixed so that it need not stand too long, and the pies 'set up' all in good time.

"Apple, berry or mince pies could be baked with bread and cake, but not many custard or pumpkin pies, because the steam arising from them would cause the bread and cake to be heavy.

"It was considered as much of a disgrace to be without pie, if a guest dropped in for dinner or supper, as without bread; and it was a common practice to bake, after the weather became cool enough so that they would keep two or three days, ten or twelve pumpkin pies at one baking."

Rye flour, rather than wheat, was the staple for bread. Wheat was generally reserved for cakes, pie crust, and "company biscuit." Corn was also used extensively.

"Hasty pudding was almost a daily food in some form at some seasons of the year, and it was expected that every miller know the best way to crack corn for samp. . .Almost as soon as the buckwheat was harvested and threshed, griddle cakes made their appearance upon the breakfast table, and regularly appeared until spring."

"Cider apple sauce," which is similar to apple butter, accompanied nearly every meal in the winter. A kind of ritual was associated with preparing the apples the evening before the apple sauce was made.

Mrs. Johnson described the importance associated with making apple sauce: "The making of it was considered of so much consequence that, when the teacher who boarded around the district, sent to see if he could go to some place, the reply sometimes came, 'Mother can't have you next week, she hain't made apples sass'."

During the summer, the only meat available was "salt pork, salt beef, ham and dried beef, with now and then a fowl from the barnyard. Of fish, there was codfish, salted mackerel, Housatonic River shad (of which most farmers laid in a supply in the spring), with now and then a mess of pan fish from the brooks."

When, some years later, a butcher's cart began to make rounds with fresh meat in the summer, "It was considered a wonderful thing," Mrs. Johnson recalled.

"The only refrigerator our mothers had was the well, and happy was the woman whose well was deep and cold and never-failing. Two or three or more pails or baskets were almost always hung in it. She depended upon it to cool her cream for churning, and to keep the butter solid for the table, as well as to preserve a little longer any fresh bit she was fortunate enough to have.

"Our mothers knew nothing of creameries or separators or cheese factories; but every woman made butter and cheese from her own dairy, often milking the cows also."

These thrifty New England farm women did not miss a chance to sell some of their homemade produce when the opportunity presented itself. During the summer a market cart went from farm to farm collecting butter, cheese, eggs, and chickens.

"The chickens were carried in a coop swung from the rear axle. The produce was taken to Bridgeport or New Haven, the returns for one week being made the next, and the housewife whose butter cleared a York shilling thought herself well off. If more than that was realized, the price was considered extra good."

Mrs. Johnson told of making candles, the only light which her mother had ever known, every spring and fall. Spinning and weaving were also done in the spring, before house-cleaning and soap-making.

"Some of our mothers knew enough of chemistry, although they did not call it that, to know what conditions were necessary to 'bring' the soap, and were almost always successful; others boiled and boiled and spent a great deal of time, and strength, and patience, with very indifferent results."

Mrs. Johnson drew a philosophical conclusion to her fond reminiscences:

"I would like once more to hear the musical whizzing of the old wool wheel, as it sounded when I was a child, and my mother kept time to its music in the long narrow kitchen of the old house at home, but I am thankful that the women of today need not tread in all the foot-steps of our mothers."

Oral History of Newtown Family Life on a Farm
by Mrs. Edward (Kate) Knapp

The early recollections of Mrs. Knapp and other long-time Newtown residents, many of which were recorded by the Newtown Historical Society during the nation's bicentennial in 1976, provide a first-hand insight into family life in the late 19th century.

These citizens grew up shortly after the turn of the 20th century, prior to the advent of the telephone, automobile, and electricity. Family life at the time had scarcely changed from the way it was lived some years earlier, during the 19th century.

Those who recall "the good old days," in writing or on tape, provide a vision of simpler, quieter and generally happy times, despite the physical demands of farm work, and the heavy toll that death continued to exert.

Mrs. Knapp moved with her family from Pound Ridge, New York, to their farm on Sherman Street in Sandy Hook when she was a baby. They arrived at the Botsford Railroad Station and walked the rest of the way. She was one of 15 brothers and sisters, several of whom died of typhoid fever.

"It was great in the old days," she recalled. "We all got along very well and never had any problems. We used to know everybody. Everyone helped one another. We never locked the door to the farmhouse.

"We went to the one room school house in the

Zoar district. You learned your lessons, or you didn't pass. Ella Lillis was our teacher. She was one wonderful teacher."

All Newtown youngsters beneath the age of 12 or 13 attended one room school houses in the town's 21 school districts which had been established in the late 18th century. The town's first public high school was built in 1902.

Her family did not have a bathroom when Mrs. Knapp was young. Rather they had a "three seater" outhouse which had two big seats and one little one for the small folks. No one seemed to mind these arrangements at the time.

"We weren't rich, but we were clean," Mrs. Knapp recalled. "We'd wear the same dress to school every day, come home, get changed, and go out to the fields to pick potatoes. Or we'd fix the garden. When we were in the garden, not being watched, we had our fun, too."

All family members, including the children, helped out with the chores. Laundry was usually done on Saturday, and had to be finished before the children could go anywhere. The older ones had to wash out the diapers. The clothes lines were filled with diapers when the children were young.

"We never said, 'no' to our parents," she remembered. "We never got whipped, either, or punished by getting hit."

When they finished their chores, the children found plenty of time to play. Hide and seek, tag, hop scotch, and "duck on the rock" were popular games with Mrs. Knapp and her numerous brothers and sisters. They also enjoyed swimming in local lakes and waterholes, and sledding and skating in the winter.

Their mother, despite her many mouths to feed and raise, enjoyed playing cards and organized many dances for the young people at her home. She also did a lot of sewing and crocheting.

"She was a devout mother," Mrs. Knapp said with utmost reverence.

Fresh milk, cheese and butter were always in abundance at their home. They made butter, "whenever there was enough cream atop the milk. We had big pans of milk which we kept in the basement where it was cool. We skimmed it and whipped the butter by hand."

The family also grew most of its own vegetables and raised cows, horses, and pigs. The pigs were butchered in the fall and the meat kept for use all winter.

"My brother used to drive cattle to Bridgeport to the slaughterhouse," she recalled. "All the roads were dirt then, even Main Street."

Mrs. Knapp went to work for the Curtiss Packaging Company in 1925, at the age of 15. She had wanted to be a nurse, but two of her sisters were involved in an automobile accident, and it was necessary for her to help out. She celebrated her 60th anniversary as an employee there.

She married Judge Edward Knapp, longtime probate judge for Newtown, who is now deceased. The couple had four children.

Oral History by Laura Mosely
Interviewed in 1976
by Jerry Jackson

Miss Laura Mosely spent three months in Newtown every summer while she was growing up around the turn of the century. Her father was President of Yale College, and her grandparents had been Newtown citizens.

She described what summer residents did for entertainment: "There were no movies. On Sunday evening my uncle's family would come walking an eighth of a mile down the road to our house. . .Uncle Charley played the guitar, and Mother played the guitar, too. . .

"We usually started out with hymns and ended up with Spanish war songs that were very far from hymns. We had a good bit of Gilbert and Sullivan that we sang, too.

"You didn't use the horses to go see your neighbors. Instead you would walk on the nice unoccupied country roads a mile or two each way just to have the pleasure of a walk and to drop in and call on your friends. It was a very leisurely kind of thing.

"We just had a tiny little porch. One of our great entertainments in thunderstorms was for us all to crowd outside on the porch and watch the lightning. It was pretty spectacular lightning.

"We used candles mainly in the bedrooms and kerosene lamps in the kitchen and living room at night. . .There was a great deal of reading aloud because you couldn't get too many people around that light. The family also played cards in the evening, poker, or solitaire or other competitive games with cards."

She told of some of the living arrangements back then: "Not having electricity, you had an ice house. There were double walls with sawdust in-between the walls. In winter, when Warner's Pond was frozen over, they cut the ice and put those huge blocks between layers of sawdust in the ice house. You had an icebox, not a refrigerator, which dripped. You had to put a pan underneath it, or pretty soon you'd have a flooded floor.

"The water supply was not much to be counted on, but thanks to the well and the outhouse, you got along alright. Every morning the maids would bring a nice little can of hot water to every room which had a pitcher and basin. The pitcher had cold water.

"You were careful about bathing, using the pitcher and basin. Every Sunday we used to go down to the Housatonic River to swim. Aunt Betty and Uncle Charley would hitch up the horse and wagon, and the two families would go down. There wasn't room for people to ride both ways.

"You could have your choice. You could walk down, and then ride back, all nice and clean. Or you could ride down in the heat of the day and walk back when the dusk was falling."

Oral History by Charles Botsford
Interviewed by Jerry Jackson

Born in 1895, Mr. Charles Botsford was the ninth generation of a family that settled in Newtown in the early 1700s. He was the last one born in the old farm house on Mt. Nebo Road. His family were dairy farmers who used to bring their milk to Stepney to sell.

He spoke of the weather conditions when he was a boy, indicating that they had changed: "We had a lot of snow in those days. Winters were cold back then. It went down to zero more often. We used a horse and sleigh all winter."

He described how the cold weather helped them keep meat over the winter: "We used to get a quarter of beef and hang it in the coldest room of the house. It would freeze solid, and we'd go and cut off a piece when we wanted it."

His family managed very well without electric-ity. "I can't think of anything that bothered us economically," he said.

"We had a root cellar where we used to keep apples, potatoes, turnips - you could walk right in. We had butchers who used to come around every week with their meat wagon. The assistant clerk at Morris's General Store would come around on Thursday and take orders and deliver groceries on Friday."

"We never had any alcohol in the house," he reported.

He, like his contemporaries and several genera-tions before him, went to the one room school house, which he described: "We used to walk over hills to the Palestine School. We had a big stove in the middle to heat the place.

"The most children that ever went there was 27. We had a full house that time. Most of the teachers were women. The teacher would call the first group in reading, the second group in reading. . .Each one would take about 15 min-utes.

"Everyone carried his or her own lunch. Some-times we used to go sledding at noon. We did a lot of sledding downhill."

Oral History by Frank Johnson
Interviewed by Jerry Jackson

Mr. Frank Johnson, a descendant of Beach Camp and some of the settlers of Newtown dating back to 1705, talked of his family life at the turn of the century. He, too, went to a one room school house. Traveling to and from school was exclusively by foot in those days.

"My education started in one of the little district schools of Newtown," he related. "It happened to be the one called South Center District School . . . a typical one room school . . . I don't remember how any teacher taught every-

Sleighing has a long tradition in Newtown. From practical winter transportation to seasonal recreation, this scene has been popular since the 18th century.

Photograph courtesy of *The Newtown Bee*

73

Frank L. Johnson, 1895-1982

photograph courtesy of Stanley King

thing to all children who were under 12 or 13 years of age.

"The benches weren't the wooden planks that were in the original school. The benches I remember were two-seaters where two people sitting at a desk had a common ink well . . .There was a rather long bench at the front of the building, near the teacher's desk, where a particular class would sit when it was reciting."

There were not as many town services then, according to Mr. Johnson. People did more themselves. There was no plowing of roads.

"During the blizzard of 1888, a train got stuck in Newtown," he related. "People helped to shovel out the train."

He recalled how they heated their home: "We had a wood burning stove in the kitchen and a heating stove in the living room. When I got up in the morning in the wintertime, the rooms upstairs were not heated."

For fun during his childhood, he recalled: "There was always the swimming hole in the summer and skating in the winter . . . We had sleds. There was a very good hill on part of our land, on what is now Elm Road."

Living on a dairy farm as he did, he learned to milk cows as a boy. His family also kept chickens and horses. "I never cared much for farming," he admitted.

—Nancy Newill Doniger

July 4, 1914, Main Street.

photograph courtesy of
The Men's Literary and Social Club of Newtown Street

part III

The Twentieth Century

Weathervane, Sandy Hook Elementary School.   photograph by Joseph I. Kugielsky

The 20th Century
Tradition Tempers Growth

*A*t the dawn of the 20th century, Newtown was very much a part of the vitality of the whole nation. Here, agriculture was still the rule, but industry was booming, aided by the new wonder of electricity. There was already talk of electric street lights, which would replace the old gas models in 1915. There were automobiles in town: Locomobiles, Victor Steamers, Ramblers, Oldsmobiles, and Stevens-Duryeas. The population of the town in 1900 was 3,276.

Newtown was preparing for a birthday. Nineteen hundred and five marked the 200th year since the land purchase from the Indians, and those in town were prepared to celebrate. In January of that year, a meeting was held in the high school to plan a bicentennial commemoration on August 5th. There would be a parade with bands, horses, floats, fire engines, and references to the Pootatuck tribe. Visiting dignitaries, including Connecticut Governor Henry Roberts, entertained the crowd with speeches.

One celebrity who was not in attendance was President Theodore Roosevelt, who had sent regrets; he was unable to leave Washington with the Russo-Japanese war in progress and plans for the Panama Canal being discussed by Congress.

Curiously, this was the second almost-visit to Newtown in this new century by the Chief Executive. *The Newtown Bee* reported a crowd of 300 assembled on September 3, 1902, to watch the President's train pass through the Newtown station. Due to an attempt on Roosevelt's life and the consequent death of a Secret Service agent earlier on the trip, plans for stops were cancelled. It was reported, however, that "President Roosevelt appeared on the rear platform of his car and bowed to the people as the train rushed by." Among those waiting for a glimpse of the great man were the children of the North Center School.

Corsets.

Corsets of all kinds at astonishingly low prices.

"GLOVE·FITTING"
PARIS SHAPE
(SHORT HIP),

Courtesy of *The Newtown Bee*

The first decade of the century brought many innovations to town. The spread of rural telephones received editorial attention in *The Newtown Bee* in March of 1905. When a new phone was installed it made front page news in the paper, and the telephone number was published for all to see.

In 1907, the Borough contracted with the Newtown Water Company to provide fire hydrants at $30 each per year.

Patent medicines purported to cure every complaint from nervousness in mothers to cancer. Alcohol and opium were often used ingredients. The consumer, however, had a new friend — the Pure Food and Drug Act was passed in 1904.

Gentlemen sported handlebar moustaches or beards. The ladies were tightly corseted, and their dresses were heavy and ornate. Voluminous overcoats covered the knees and legs for protection in open, unheated buggies or cars. Sateen skirts in "colors and black" were advertised at the Brick Store in Sandy Hook.

A popular annual event was the Newtown Agricultural Society Fair. The fairgrounds, on land that would later include Taylor Field behind the Hawley School, included an oval track for trotting races, parades, oxen pulls, and poultry exhibits. The fair was greatly missed when it was discontinued in 1906.

Temperance, a movement active in Newtown since an 1854 state grant for local efforts against the evils of drink, was still of major interest to many citizens. Those who voted against the 1919 Prohibition amendment were listed in the *Bee*. Vigilance continued into the abstinence years with tales of "beer runners" caught transporting their cargo through town.

Women's suffrage was also on the minds of many townspeople. Prominent citizens formed the Equal Franchise League and, in 1915, the newspaper printed an editorial urging state legislators to vote in favor of suffrage for Connecticut's women.

A letter entitled "Ten Questions" and signed simply A.S.B., in the April 16, 1915, *Bee* detailed the popular arguments against women's suffrage and asked questions about their validity:

> Here are some common sense questions to which it is claimed that no opponent of suffrage has ever given a satisfactory answer:
> 1. If equal suffrage is so bad a thing, why has it spread from the State that first adopted it to ten neighboring States, all adjoining one another?
> 2. If the majority of the people anywhere are dissatisfied with it, why is there no move to repeal it?

3. If it leads mothers to neglect their children, why is the lowest infant death rate in the world found in New Zealand? [New Zealand had granted women the right to vote.]

4. If it increases divorce, why did Colorado grant 935 divorces the year before women were given the ballot and only 597 the year after?

5. If it is demoralizing, why did only 62 out of 624 ministers and editors in the Suffrage States replying to Julia Ward Howe's letter of inquiry give an unfavorable opinion?

6. If the majority of women are opposed, why have only about one per cent of the women in the United States joined the widely-advertised National Association Opposed to Women's Suffrage, according to that association's own records?

7. If the majority of women are opposed in Massachusetts where an active Anti-Suffrage Association has been gathering signatures of women against suffrage since 1895, why has it succeeded in 20 years in accumulating the names of only about three per cent of the women of the state?

8. Among the millions of citizens in the enfranchised States, why have the opponents of equal suffrage thus far failed to find a dozen respectable men who assert over their own names and addresses that it has had any bad results?

9. From the largest Chamber of Commerce to the smallest sewing circle, why has no organization of any kind in a suffrage state ever passed a resolution condemning it?

10. Unless most people like it after they have experience of it, why do opponents warn us that, once granted, it can never be recalled?

Women first voted in the Newtown elections of October, 1920.

20th Century Economy: Reflecting the Town's Changing Character

Turn-of-the-century factories flourishing along the town's rivers and rail lines were certainly a welcome aspect of Newtown's economy. These ranged from the button shops and mills along the Pootatuck and its branches in Botsford and Sandy Hook, to Hawleyville's Upham factory. Here the tea ball (later referred to as tea bag) was invented in 1909, and "100 lbs. of peanut butter a day" were produced in 1916.

Controversy over the desirability of these and more incoming businesses has been a recurring point of discussion among townspeople. As early as 1919, *The Newtown Bee* printed an editorial letter by W. J. McLaughlin, who felt that Newtown had both space and resources for great expansion. In his enthusiasm for Newtown-as-an-industrial-center, Mr. McLaughlin described the potential: "Main Street would tremble under the weight of traffic, so that Fifth Avenue and 42nd Street would seem to have been transported to our fair domain."

It seems that few of his neighbors wished to see their green and rural home trans-formed into a rival of New York City. Throughout the 20th century the reputation

Courtesy of *The Newtown Bee*

of commuter haven that Mr. McLaughlin so bemoaned has gained strength.

Despite evidence and arguments to the contrary, Newtown was still, during the first third of the new century, an agricultural town. It was, however, getting harder and harder to eke a living from the land and resist the real estate values.

The farmer found that the war years of 1916-18 were to initiate a wide gap between inflation and market prices which would escalate and threaten his way of life.

In February of 1919, the *Bee* reported that the cost of "the things which the the Farmer buys have increased 102%, while the things he sells have increased 71%, or a difference of 31% on the purchasing dollar."

By the mid 1920s, a growing and restless population in New York City and nearby Westchester County discovered the benefits of Newtown for summer homes and vacations. Farms were passing to the ownership of outsiders, and vacation lot communities began to appear. Land along Lake Zoar (formed by the Stevenson Dam project begun in 1918), the Housatonic, and the Pootatuck Rivers, became prime real estate. Three enterprising Bridgeport businessmen bought 100 acres and developed Shady Rest, declared a "summer paradise" by 1925. Afterward came Riverside, which was advertised as "filling up" in 1926, and then the Cedarhurst community.

Newtown, Conn.

GRAND CENTRAL HOTEL.

postcards courtesy of Melissa Houghton

The summer boom of the "roaring 20s" also brought business to the inns that had served Newtown since stagecoach days. There was great activity in the hotel business, both on Main Street and at the railway station sites. In 1925, the Grand Central Hotel changed ownership and became the Parker House. (This was a popular tourist and town gathering spot; it later became the Yankee Drover Inn. A Newtown landmark, the building survived several earlier blazes but was completely destroyed in a fire on January 18, 1981.)

"Tea Houses" were springing up all over town. These genteel-sounding establishments had names such as the Betsy Page, Old Orchard, the Little Brown House, Sophie's, Glen Brook, and the Maryland. Although they changed hands and sometimes names, these businesses survived well into the depression years. Some, in fact, including the Flagpole Fountain Lunch and the Log Cabin (which later became the Fireside Inn), were opened during that slow economic time.

Newtown was spared the worst economic ills of the depression. Due to the continuing demand for relatively inexpensive summer and permanent housing for commuters, property values held, and the town's population was on the rise again after a 1900-1930 decline.

As in most rural areas, the self-sufficiency inherent in an agriculture-based economy enabled Newtown's citizens to survive — not without hardship, but at least without the dire poverty experienced by many inner city dwellers.

The town had a surprise asset which helped in hard times: the generosity of Mary Elizabeth Hawley. Her first major gift to the town came in 1922, when The Hawley School was dedicated. Before her death in 1930, Miss Hawley would provide the gates and receiving vault at the Village Cemetery, and give her hometown its government center. As with the school, the Edmond Town Hall donation included land, building, and an endowment for maintenance.

In her will, similar arrangements were stipulated for a new library and a war monument. At a time when most towns and cities in America could not afford a new building for any purpose, Newtown was breaking ground.

One sign of some economic decline in town was reflected by the discontinuation of passenger rail service. By 1930, there were complaints of unreliable schedules and services on the railways. That year, one fewer train stopped at the Hawleyville station. Further reductions followed until the once bustling Hawleyville stop was closed completely in 1932. Automobile and bus competition were irreversible, and all passenger service to Newtown was abandoned in 1936.

Although industry was still serviced by freight lines, the loss of passenger

—continued page 88

VERANDA
NEWTOWN INN
NEWTOWN,
CONN.

83

Upham's Japanese Tea Garden

Unique among Newtown's tea houses was W. A. Upham's Japanese Tea Garden in Hawleyville. Mr. Upham had been a pioneer in the tea industry, so it was appropriate that he devise this ambitious project as described on its opening in June of 1928 by *The Newtown Bee*:

> *The tea house is being most attractively fitted up. On the south side will be an enclosed dining porch. Inside will be a reception room and private dining room and on the north side a Japanese gift room fitted with oriental furnishing and novel and beautiful Japanese gift articles.*
>
> *This is not a business but just a plaything with Upham but he expects it will go over big. The lake at night when it is illuminated by the electric lights certainly presents a beautiful appearance.*

The garden lake had been specially dredged and was spanned by rustic bridges. Canoes and a rowboat were available for use by customers. In front of the tea house stood the life-size figure of a Chinese mandarin (which would be destroyed by anti-Japanese vandals during World War II).

Thirty-two large catalpa trees were added to the landscape in 1929, and, in 1930, the lake was extended. An island was created on which was presented the largest miniature golf course in Connecticut at the time.

Mr. Upham's expectations were fulfilled. Authentic or not, the Japanese Tea Garden was a big success. Over the next several years, the local newspaper carried reports from the tea house of civic and organizational meetings that had previously been held exclusively at the dining establishments of downtown Newtown.

84

photographs courtesy of Priscilla and John Cascone

Mary Elizabeth Hawley

"She built for the future in her own way, in her own town. That was her ambition and her dream." These words were spoken in eulogy at the 1930 funeral of Mary Elizabeth Hawley, one of the most distinguished, generous, and mysterious citizens in Newtown's history.

Mary Elizabeth was of the ninth generation in descent from Joseph Hawley, who sailed from England in 1650 to settle in Stratford, Connecticut. Her father, Marcus Clinton Hawley, was an astute businessman who was associated with a family hardware business in Bridgeport. Sensing the needs of an expanding nation, he made a fortune in hardware and agricultural implements. He foresaw the development of the West and invested accordingly in railroads, steamship lines, and water works. At one time, Marcus Hawley served as president of two railroads, a steamship company, and a major water company. Probably Newtown's first entrepreneur, he amassed an immense fortune.

Born in Bridgeport in 1834, Marcus married Sarah Booth, and together they settled in the Booth family home in Newtown. He cut a dashing figure as he commuted daily to his offices in Bridgeport or New York, driving to the Newtown Railroad Station in a two-wheeled gig with a pair of sprightly Dalmatians running under it.

In 1857 Mary Elizabeth was the first child born to Marcus and Sarah. Three brothers followed, but two died in early childhood and the third, William, lived only until his 16th year. Before his untimely death, William apparently attended Yale for a few months. This connection may account for the significant bequests that Miss Hawley made to that University many years later.

Mary ("Mame" to her family) apparently grew up along strictly conventional lines in a period of great conservatism. In her youth, she cut a very striking figure in her tiny-waisted Victorian dresses, some of which have been preserved along with a monogrammed, sterling-silver

photograph courtesy of *The Newtown Bee*

capped riding crop in the Cyrenius H. Booth Library historical collections. Her youthful Newtown activities seem to have been centered around affairs at the Congregational Church, which she attended regularly.

As rumors often surround the private lives of wealthy and prominent figures, local legends have been woven concerning a possible 1885 marriage between Miss Hawley and the Reverend Mr. J. Addison Crockett.

Like a plot straight out of a Victorian novel, rumor claimed that Mary Elizabeth married this young man, who was serving as temporary minister of Trinity Episcopal Church, and sailed off with him for a European honeymoon. The mystery deepened and the plot thickened when her parents sailed for Europe shortly after the presumed wedding and brought Mary home — alone. Whatever the truth behind this story of her ill-fated love, it is certain that in Newtown she remained Mary Elizabeth Hawley and thereafter lived nearly as a recluse with her father and mother in their home on Newtown Street (later know as Main Street or Route 25).

Her father died in 1899, and she and her mother lived an even more cloistered existence, venturing out for walks only after dark. Neighborhood tales were told about the extreme parsimony of old Mrs. Hawley: Mary Elizabeth had to patch and repatch her clothing; only at the doctor's insistence three days before her death did her mother begrudgingly allow installation of a telephone.

As the years passed, Mary Elizabeth assumed some of her father's features — a heavy frame and features and a short neck. By the time Mrs. Hawley died in 1920 at the age of 90, Mary Elizabeth was 63 years old.

With the encouragement of a long-time friend and financial advisor, Arthur T. Nettleton, Miss Hawley enthusiastically made some modern improvements in her home. She sported new clothes and invested in a handsome Pierce-Arrow automobile for daily excursions. At this point in her life and at the urging of Mr. Nettleton, she looked about her and recognized the needs of her community.

So began a decade of philanthropy that was to alter the face of Newtown. An editorial at the time of her death stated, "She did not give to far away institutions to make her name big in the world. She chose instead to benefit her home town and make it more beautiful."

First came her 1922 gift of Hawley School. This was the first public building in Newtown to have central heating (with coal), indoor plumbing, a gymnasium, and an auditorium. She provided a trust fund for maintenance, the purchase of coal, and the employment of a custodian.

Newtown's benefactress then turned her attention to the Village Cemetery where she funded preservation of the old, pre-revolutionary section. She planned and financed imposing front gates and a memorial vault and then saw to the building of a bridge leading to the cemetery entrance. In 1928, she had a lake, which was later christened Hawley Pond, excavated at the foot of the bridge, making the area "one of the most beautiful God's Acres in Connecticut," according to a local minister of the day.

Edmond Town Hall, named after her great grandfather Judge William Edmond, was next on Miss Hawley's schedule. The handsome architecture of this building made it one of Connecticut's public showplaces. For many years, Edmond Town Hall served as the center of activity in Newtown — with its movie theater, bowling alley, post office, ballroom (the Alexandria Room) with fully equipped kitchen facilities, and the town government offices.

Although it was Mary Elizabeth's wish to have one of those new talking pictures in the building so that she might walk up the street to enjoy a film, she would not live to see the opening of either the town hall or the theater. As one of her last official acts, however, she was able to lay the cornerstone.

Mary Elizabeth Hawley died on May 11, 1930, about three months before the scheduled town hall dedication. A great crowd gathered for the funeral. A long cortege proceeded from her home on Main Street, down Sugar Street, and to the Village Cemetery on Elm Drive. The town's flags flew at half staff, and the bell atop Edmond Town Hall, ringing for the first time, tolled. An entire town mourned for the lady whose good deeds were done in a quiet way.

Five months later, the reading of Miss Hawley's will revealed further plans — for a library to be named after her grandfather Cyrenius H. Booth and for a Soldiers and Sailors Monument to commemorate Newtown's war dead. These projects were completed in 1932 and 1939, respectively.

A grateful town honored Mary Elizabeth Hawley. A special town meeting was called just to pay tribute to her memory, and townspeople set about raising money to commission a portrait of their benefactress. Over 1,270 people, including school children with pennies, donated to the fund.

The portrait, painted by F. Sexton, was unveiled on the first anniversary of the Edmond Town Hall dedication, a date that would also have been Mary Elizabeth's birthday, August 22, 1931. The portrait, which became a centerpiece in the Mary Hawley Room of the town hall, was flanked by two large baskets of red flowers to match the red velvet dress in which Miss Hawley had been depicted.

Some mysteries about the upbringing and private life of Mary Elizabeth Hawley have remained unsolved. The benefits to Newtown of her generosity, however, were never in question. In an editorial at the time of her death, *The Newtown Bee* commented on the character revealed in her use of great wealth: "Mary Elizabeth Hawley truly wrought nobly, thoughtfully and well for her native community."

— Mae S. Schmidle

photograph courtesy of *The Newtown Bee*
Cyrenius H. Booth Library, Main Street.

photographs by Ken Kast

Storm Ridge Farm

When Dennis Sisco and his wife Alexine Lesko found a very special ridge site that was once part of a Newtown farm, they determined to have a house built that was worthy of the view.

As a result, William Grover and Stephen Lloyd of Centerbrook Architects were chosen to design a house that would be modern and spacious inside while fitting comfortably into the natural beauty of a New England country setting.

Storm Ridge house, the solution, has a French Provincial look, with two nearly separate wings connected in original and unusual ways. The interior is full of open spaces, with high ceilings and numerous windows spaced to act as frames for the most spectacular views. The house and grounds were featured in the August, 1988 issue of *Architectural Digest*.

Built between April, 1985 and June, 1986, Storm Ridge Farm may not qualify as an historical Newtown house. It is, however, a triumph of design that combines modern and traditional beauty in a unique way.

traffic was to signal a marked deterioration in the vacation business. The "summer people" tended to go elsewhere — or to buy their Newtown property and stay for longer periods or move to the town permanently.

By 1931, the borough had passed new zoning laws that affected the industrial scene. Newtown's residential potential was already recognized, as was the importance of maintenance of the traditional rural character. Traffic was a problem in both Newtown and Sandy Hook, and roads were still unpaved. Not until 1934 did the town apply for grants to put down hard surface roads.

The borough especially was gaining an awareness of the stress put on a town by growth. Concerns over adequate water supplies, sewers, trash dumping, and transportation availability made zoning a necessity.

In 1928, Connecticut located Fairfield Hills in Newtown. Patients and staff of this mental treatment facility would swell the borough population yet again.

Although the town as a whole began debating the desirability of establishing overall zoning regulations by the early 1940s, it was not until 1955 that a Planning Commission was elected to oversee the development of a comprehensive plan for growth. A year later, the town created a joint Planning and Zoning Commission with a Zoning Board of Appeals.

By this time, the die was cast. Because of its location near the Long Island Sound area, Newtown avoided the congestion of the industrial areas but enjoyed the advantage of accessibility. Rimmed by the manufacturing centers of Ansonia-Derby, Bridgeport, and Waterbury, and within commuting distance of lower Fairfield County and New York City, Newtown's position was directly in the path of the suburban movement.

In 1930, Newtown's population was 2,635 — very nearly identical to that of 1775. By 1960, the number had increased to 8,393 and leaped to over 17,000 by the National Bicentennial year of 1976.

During all this building and residential upheaval, industry took second place in Newtown's economy. The old factories along the Pootatuck held on, changed owners and functions, and were eventually closed or converted into office buildings for the growing number of professional and service-oriented businesses.

In the 1960s and 70s some companies were established in a new industrial park on Commerce Road to take advantage of the proximity of the new route I-84. These years, however, generally saw a decline in the family factories and signaled an exodus of many of the working class descendants of Sandy Hook's immigrant population.

In 1977 the old Fabric Hose Company closed its doors. It sat empty until 1980, when, after gaining a listing in the National Register of Historic Places, new owners began a restoration project that would convert the still-handsome brick structure into a light industry and office building. Similar plans were made for the "upper mill."

In 1981, the Curtis family ended a five-generation tradition when it sold its Berkshire business to five former employees.

There were survivors. The general stores adapted to the needs of the suburban population, providing everything from delicatessan service to video rentals.

Main Street, circa 1940s.

photograph courtesy of *The Newtown Bee*

Another success story has been *The Newtown Bee*. Retained by the Smith family throughout the century, it grew to be a true regional weekly. Offices were moved in 1903 to Church Hill Road and were expanded in 1950. A critically acclaimed "Antiques" section later became a separate publication with subscribers from all over the nation.

In 1977, the *Bee* celebrated 100 years in Newtown. This local newspaper, cited by *The Bridgeport Herald* in 1928 as "the most unique country weekly," and remembered fondly by the likes of James Thurber, holds a very special place as participant in and chronicler of Newtown history.

W. A. Honan General Store and Post Office, Hawleyville.

Newtown Farmers in the Great Depression

Dairy farming was generally a family business. Charles D. Ferris Jr., born in 1902, and Donald B. Ferris, born in 1904, spent their youth working on their father's 230-acre farm. (Originally purchased in 1854, the farm, "Ferris Acres," located on Route 302, is still being operated by the Ferris family.) As a natural course, the two brothers followed in their father's footsteps. According to them, they chose to dairy farm because it was what they liked and knew best. To them there was no other suitable way of life, in spite of the hardships. Charles Jr. continued with his father, while Donald went out on his own in 1928. Charles and his father had 20 cows in 1922; Donald began with 12. Both herds continued to grow. They marketed the milk to Blinkey Dairy in Bridgeport and later joined the Connecticut Milk Producers Association (CMPA), a Connecticut farmer-owned cooperative.

The Boyson family began farming on a 110 acre dairy farm in the Palestine district of Newtown in 1882. In 1912, the Boyson family moved to a 30-acre farm near the town's center. Boyson had planned to retire, but he purchased a Jersey cow for his wife. That one cow began a milk delivery business satisfying neighbors' demand for fresh milk. By 1925, the herd had grown to 20 cows and the Boysons were delivering milk to 800 Newtown customers.

Stephen Paproski was an immigrant from the Ukraine. After working for ACME Shearing Company in Bridgeport, he came to Newtown where he met his bride-to-be. Soon the couple bought a dozen and a half cows and rented a Newtown farm. Paproski purchased a small farm near Toddy Hill, and, in 1925, he purchased an 84-acre farm in the Palestine district, which his brother operated. Nine years later he sold it again for twice the price, bought Castle Hill Farm on Route 302, and moved his herd of 50 cows there. The Paproskis sold their milk to independent dealers and later delivered to customers in Bridgeport.

The Kearns family began farming in Newtown in 1936 on a 98 acre farm on Bennett's Bridge Road in Sandy Hook. Florence Kearns, her father — a dairyman from Danbury — and her husband — a dairyman from New York — had previously been farming in New York State. The New York farm had no electricity, but the one on Bennett's

photograph by Pat McNally

Bridge did. The Kearns sold their milk to independent dealers but later switched to CMPA.

Modernization varied from farm to farm, but by the mid-1930s most of Newtown dairy farms had electricity used for milking, cooling the milk, and lighting barns. Before the introduction of electricity in rural areas it took two men two and a half hours to milk 20 cows by hand. Farmers milked twice each day in dim stables by gas light or kerosene lanterns. In winter months the stable had to be cleaned by hand every day.

Horses and oxen were the beasts of burden on Newtown's dairy farms until gas engine tractors slowly took over their duties. Farmers used single horses or teams to plow, cut, rake, and "tedd" hay (a drying process where the hay is fluffed up to air out), and to pull wagon loads of forage and produce.

Small concerns such as the 30-acre Boyson farm bought most of the hay and corn used to feed animals, while large farms produced corn, hay, and other feed crops. The farmer used a horse-

91

Photographs taken at Kearns' Farm by Pat McNally.

drawn plow or tractor to turn over his corn field. Stephen Paproski's son Henry recalls that, during the 1930s, farmers used to plow their corn fields earlier in the year. The stubble left over from the previous harvest had to be plowed under before the corn borer could take hold in the soil. (*The Newtown Bee* reported a corn borer epidemic in April, 1932, which caused a quarantine in Newtown.)

The farmer marked his corn field lengthways and crossways and planted seed at each intersection. Mrs. Kearns remembers that it took two men two days to plant their five acre corn field by hand, carrying the sack of seed on their backs. Most dairy farmers used a horse-drawn cultivator to cut up the grass or weeds that could cause

malignity in the corn. The trained horse walked so as not to pull the cultivator over the rows. The corn fields also had to be hoed once or twice until the time came to cut the stalks with a corn knife.

In the 1930s most farms stored their corn in a wooden silo. Some farmers ran the stalks through a gasoline belt driven blower which blew the chopped plant into the silo. Leftover corn was stored out in the fields in "stouts," corn stalks packed together vertically.

Charles Ferris remembered a hurricane in 1938 which swept through Newtown with strong winds and heavy rains, destroying nearly half his farm's corn crop. He used a hand-turned corn sheller to remove the kernels from the fallen corn cobs and fed them to his pigs. The empty cobs

were then taken to a gristmill to make cobmeal.

Charles and his father also raised two acres of oats. At harvest time they cut and "cradled" the oats by hand. A gasoline powered thrashing machine processed the oats. Cobmeal and oats were mixed and fed to horses.

Farmers used a horse-drawn or tractor-pulled mower to cut their hay. If the weather was dry and sunny, the hay would be ready the next day. It had to be "fluted" or turned in the field with a pitchfork or horse-drawn "tedder" that kicked the hay high into the air. The farmer raked the hay with a truck. Workers stomped and packed the loose hay tightly until they achieved a firm load. Eva Ferris remembered the discomfort she experienced stomping hay while wearing a long dress and stockings.

Most of the dairy farmers stored their hay in a barn and sometimes stacked extra in the field. The finished teepee-shaped hay stack shed water and kept the hay until needed. Charles Ferris said he had to build fences around the stacks to prevent the cows from helping themselves.

Dairy farmers used cow manure to fertilize their crops. The farmer loaded the manure onto a wagon and spread it in the fields with a pitch fork. Some farmers owned a labor-saving machine which spread the manure mechanically. By the 1930s many used commercial fertilizer or manufactured plant food, in addition to manure, to increase fertility of the soil. They often added two pounds of super phosphate per cow to the manure. This benefited the soil in two ways: it added necessary phosphates the manure lacked and prevented natural loss of nitrogen. Horse-drawn wooden fertilizer spreaders were also used to apply the fertilizer directly. Newtown farmers often pooled their money to purchase a commercial spreader and then shared its use.

If an animal got sick and they could not treat it themselves, the farmers called "Doc " Knapp and "Doc" Kersey, veterinarians from Danbury, but that was costly and as a last resort. Penicillin

The Paproski's "Castle Hill Farm" has become a part of the hillside landscape.

and vaccinations, later developed for many bovine diseases such as brucellosis and tuberculosis, had not been developed by the 1930s. Farmers used remedies such as raw eggs, cocoa, and browned baking flour to treat animals with digestive upsets.

A cow that calved often came down with a calcium deficiency called "milk fever," which the farmer treated by pumping air into her udder. The air-filled udder would not produce milk and kept the body's calcium in her system. Local farm product stores provided veterinary supplies that the farmer also used to treat sick animals.

Grain was a major expense for dairy farmers. They purchased it from Holcomb in Newtown, Eastern States in Bethel, or Big Y feed stores in Stepney, New Milford, and Danbury. Charles Ferris remembered feeding the cows stale bread soaked in water to eke out the grain supply during the 1930s and minimize the feed bill.

Feed companies delivered the grain in bags made of cotton cloth. The material used for these and also chicken feed bags were quite pretty and

each had a unique design. Eva Ferris used them to make aprons or curtains. Henry Paproski's mother used the lining of the grain bags as improvised cheese cloth for making cottage cheese.

After milking the cows, the farmer transferred the milk from pails to 40-quart stainless steel cans. Before electric coolers came into use, the cans were cooled in cold water springs on the farms. In the warmer months they were dipped in cold water and ice baths. The Ferrises cut ice blocks from ponds in the winter. The blocks were then drawn on a horse sleigh to the cellar of an old house where they were packed tightly with sawdust. The ice did not melt, even on the warmest days. Donald Ferris recalled going to his father's farm to get ice in the middle of summer to cool his milk.

In the 1920s, the Ferrises and many other farm families, loaded their milk cans onto their horse-drawn wagons and brought them to the center of town where a horse and wagon (later a truck) waited to bring the milk to Bridgeport's dairies.

Donald Ferris recalled digging his way through deep snow, his horse trampling drifts, in order to get to town. By the 1930s, milk trucks picked the product up at the individual farms.

The Boyson and Paproski families delivered their milk to customers' doors in quart milk bottles. These bottles had to be cleaned with hot water and "caustics" (an acidic cleaner). Bottle caps were continually revolutionized as sanitation methods improved. The Boysons delivered their milk to Newtown residents by horse and wagon and later by truck for ten cents a quart. During the worst of the depression, they had to "carry" some of their customers. In 1934 the Paproskis' began delivering to Bridgeport for twelve cents a quart.

Newtown dairymen had an excellent market for their milk whether they sold it to CMPA, independent dealers, or retail customers. The Kearns and the Ferrises were members of CMPA in the 1930s because, they said, it gave them security. Independent dealers could refuse to take their milk without warning, while the cooperative guaranteed to find a market for their product. While independent dealers sometimes paid more, the risk of losing an outlet was too great. CMPA paid an average of eight to ten cents a quart, but in 1932 they paid as little as two cents for a quart of milk.

Farmers who sold directly to retail customers received the most money for their milk, but they were subject to more frequent inspections. The state milk inspector visited every farm in Newtown twice a year, taking a milk sample and inspecting the barns and stables for overall cleanliness. The inspector also blood tested the herd for "bangs disease" and tuberculosis.

When occasionally a cow was found to have TB, the animal had to be slaughtered and the stable disinfected. The state reimbursed the farmer for the value of the cow, but he still suffered a heavy loss in milk production. Donald Ferris lost five cows in the 1930s. The Kearns lost two or three. Mr. Boyson bought some cattle from a dealer in the 1930s. Though the animals appeared healthy, blood tests indicated they had tuberculosis, and the dealer was obliged to repay the farmer.

Farm foreclosures during the depression were uncommon but they did occur, and when farmers sold there was a ready market. A band leader from New York State bought an 84 acre farm from Stephen Paproski to use as a summer home. Another farm of approximately 85 acres sold for about $8,500 during the depression, and Newtown land records show similar sales to other New Yorkers.

Dairymen supplemented their income with off-farm work. Charles Ferris Jr. and his father hauled brush and cleaned roads for $1 a day, and raised cattle and swine for Danbury markets. Donald Ferris and his father brought apples to market in Bridgeport, rising at 3 a.m. to get the cows milked first. Mr. Kearns sold cedar trees to the state for planting along the Merritt Parkway. He received $98, which paid the land taxes that year.

The farmers' wives contributed by making homemade butter, cheese, and canned fruits and vegetables from the garden to stretch the grocery dollar. Mrs. Kearns delivered eggs to a small German community near their Zoar area farm. Charles Ferris's mother Ophelia used to make nine loaves of bread for the family, and his wife Eva raised chickens and bartered eggs to a nearby market in return for groceries for her family.

Farm help was scarce in Newtown during the depression. Farmers hired wandering men whom they often referred to as "bums" to help with chores, and paid them $1 a day, sometimes with board. Donald Ferris provided hard cider in addition to the $1 as an extra incentive. The Paproskis paid $10 a month plus room and board for their hired help.

The philosophy of most Newtown dairy farmers was that you could make a living on the farm, even during the depression. If the taxes, the grain bill and the electric bill could be paid virtually everything "could be taken care of from there", they agreed. Mrs. Kearns said they never had "anything fancy" but "they managed." She told of relatives in Brooklyn, New York, who were unemployed and in a terrible state. The Kearns were happy that they were able to put food on the table. With savings, and living off the land as nearly as possible, the Kearns and the Ferrises said they made a decent living as dairy farmers.

In fact, the arrival of modern technology attracted new industries and people to Newtown, creating a stable economy for its dairy farmers. The growing local market, along with improved farm technology, enabled the family farms to become more productive and cost efficient.

In 1935, six years after the stock market crash, some 65 dairy farms made up the largest division of agriculture in Newtown. Over 1600 cows produced over a million gallons of milk. Newtown's future agriculturalists displayed their optimism that this industry would remain strong in Newtown by chartering a local Future Farmers of America chapter.

—Colleen Ferris Kimball

photograph by Pat McNally

"Ferris Acres" has been farmed since 1854 by the Ferris family.

Education: Competing in a Modern World

The progress of education closely paralleled the growth of Newtown's economy in the 20th century — and its population.

By 1900, dissatisfaction with the many school districts in town was nearly universal. Private institutions had been established for those who wanted to improve on the district curriculum or to continue to a higher academic level. Townspeople were beginning to realize that the expense of staffing and equipping so many regional schoolhouses was prohibitive — not to mention the impossibility of guaranteeing any degree of academic consistency for graduates.

The need for consolidation and a free public high school was so obvious by 1902 that the town voted to rent part of the privately-owned Newtown Academy building to establish Newtown High School. This vote was followed shortly by a mandate to consolidate all the school districts. Newtown's taxpayers, however, objected to the price of teachers' salaries and maintenance costs of new buildings. Funds were never fully appropriated. As a result, in 1916, Connecticut issued an evaluation disapproving the town's school system.

At this low point in the educational history, many parents withdrew their children from the public institutions and again formed schools of their own. Soon riding to the rescue, however, was Miss Hawley and her gift of Hawley School, which opened in 1922. In this building, all the district schools were consolidated with the high school.

In its days as a secondary school Hawley offered the only vocational agricultural course in Fairfield County. A small white building

photograph by William R. Greene

photograph by William R. Greene

photograph by Linda Napier

photograph by Linda Napier

photograph by William R. Greene

adjacent to the main building was opened in 1942 to house the Domestic Science Department and eventually the seventh grade as well. An addition of 10 classrooms, a teachers' room, a health room, and music rooms was completed in 1948. In 1953, the high school on Queen Street was completed, and grades seven through twelve moved around the corner. Hawley became the town's elementary school.

Crowding in Hawley forced the reopening of the old Sandy Hook schoolhouse. At one time, this structure housed all of the third grade students in Newtown. A new building was constructed in 1956 and was later expanded. In 1973, two slabs of granite with depressed dinosaur footprints were moved to the school grounds from Rocky Hill State Park. Large green footprints subsequently became the mascot and symbol of Sandy Hook Elementary School.

Burgeoning population led to two additional elementary school locations between 1960 and 1980. Middle Gate School was completed in 1965 in response to a need so intense that the financial appropriation was passed at a town meeting with only one dissenting vote.

Onto the grounds of this new school, set back from Route 25 in Botsford, the PTA and Newtown Historical Society moved the restored original 1850 red Middle Gate Schoolhouse.

In 1970, the town voted to empower the Board of Education to acquire a site for a fourth elementary school on Boggs Hill Road. After a lengthy court battle concerning Newtown's right (under the law of eminent domain) to locate the school

photograph by William R. Greene

photograph courtesy *The Newtown Bee*

photograph courtesy *The Newtown Bee*

photograph by William R. Greene

photograph by *The Newtown Bee*

97

there, the Connecticut Supreme Court decided in the town's favor, and Head O' Meadow School was constructed and opened in 1977.

The combined middle and high school also fell victim to overcrowding. Double sessions of classes were held in the late 1960s until completion of the new Newtown High School. This modern building, located in the Berkshire section of Sandy Hook, opened in September of 1970. Financing for special features like a large auditorium and a swimming pool was secured by a private donation from businessman Otto Heise and by agreement that these facilities would be available for use by all towns-people.

Private schools founded after the turn-of-the-century consolidation have tended to fulfill the needs of those who desire a religious education orientation and for pre-schoolers. St. Rose of Lima Catholic Church opened St. Rose School in 1958 to educate students through the eighth grade. Various nursery schools have provided early education and social contact for the growing numbers of the very young in town. The Newtown Montessori School was established in 1969, initially serving pre-kindergarten pupils but later expanding to include elementary grades as well.

The academic and curriculum goals of Newtown's schools have changed with the times. Agricultural studies gave way to courses designed to prepare students for the business world and continued study in college. The quality of the school system had much to do with attracting the affluent home buyers who increased Newtown's population so dramatically in the latter half of the century.

Newtown's system became known for its special-needs academic program and interscholastic sports records. The music department gained special respect for its excellence. Newtown's high school band and chorus entertained audiences up and down the East Coast of the U. S. and Canada. The band initiated periodic tours to the capitals of Western and Eastern Europe. In 1989, the touring Newtown High School Choir and Chorus introduced a bit of Newtown to the U.S.S.R.

Inflation and growing awareness of fiscal responsibility kept the taxpayers of Newtown wary of increased spending. Each new school building or expansion project of the 20th century was accompanied by protests and appropriation battles, and each yearly school budget was reviewed carefully with an eye to what could be pared. Just as on entry to the 20th century, the education system of Newtown approaches the 21st century in controversy and struggle.

Edmond Town Hall, Main Street.   photograph by Ken Kast

Keeping up with the demands of a rapidly increasing population proved to be a challenge for Newtown's traditionally small town New England governmental system. As in every other category of Newtown history, town government's 20th century evolution has been a tale of controversy and struggle: desire to retain the conservative rural character and tradition of colonial times combined with determination to serve the needs of an increasingly sophisticated society.

Two very significant alterations of the town's political and governmental system occurred in the 20th century. First, the town established a charter independent from the State of Connecticut. Some years later, a second dramatic change instituted Newtown's Legislative Council. Although the settlement of Newtown had acquired "town" status upon petition to the state in 1708, and although its government was established at the time of its incorporation in 1711, true legislative power remained with the Connecticut legislature until 1957. In that year the state general assembly passed legislation permitting towns to adopt charters and thus take full responsibility for "home rule."

Response was immediate. A Newtown Charter Commission was set up, and the town's first charter was adopted by an overwhelmingly favorable vote (1,312 to 123) on October 9, 1961, to become effective May 30, 1962.

Newtown's charter set forth the rights, obligations, and powers of the town, prescribed local elections and voting districts, and outlined the duties of the Board of Selectmen and all elective, appointive, and administrative officials. It defined the legislative parameters of the town meeting and made provision for taxation and management of finances.

Charter revisions began within a year. A major change, accepted by voters on November 6, 1974, was the second great alteration in the town's method of operation. Effective January 5, 1976, Newtown's government would expand to include the Legislative Council. Elected by district, this body assumed certain budgetary and legislative powers. Continuing were the Board of Selectmen, the town meeting (required for major financial decisions such as the annual budget) and the referendum with its citizens' appeal function. A Board of Ethics was also established.

After the adoption of the town charter in the early 1960s, a number of boards and commissions were named to provide for town planning, conservation and development of natural resources and open spaces, and the welfare and protection of citizens and property. Already established were the Board of Town Hall Managers (1931), the Cyrenius H. Booth Library Board (1932), and the Planning and Zoning Commission and the Zoning Board of Appeals (1956). New bodies included the Parks and Recreation Commission (1962), the Conservation Commission (1963), the Police Commission (1971), and the Committee on Aging (1973). Members of boards and commissions were either elected or appointed. All positions were unsalaried.

The rising number of residents and visitors in Newtown made obvious by mid-century the need for extended police and fire protection. Before 1962, there was a resident Connecticut State Police Sergeant and a local constabulary, the members of which were paid on a fee basis for traffic direction and arrests.

By 1971, a force of 19 policemen and a chief was in operation. That year, the Police Commission was appointed and charged with organizing a new Police Department and hiring a Chief of Police. The Dog Warden was also placed under Police Commission jurisdiction.

Since its founding in 1803, the Newtown Hook and Ladder Company with its corps of volunteers had served as the town's only fire fighters. One company in such a (geographically) large town soon became overburdened when faced with the busy 20th century.

Thus it was that the Dodgingtown Volunteer Fire Company was formed in 1911 and the Hawleyville Volunteer Fire Company in 1925. Sandy Hook Volunteers organized on a local level in 1937. The United Fire Company of Botsford became the town's fifth volunteer group in 1949.

Members of all these organizations donated their time and risked their lives for the citizens of Newtown. These dedicated volunteers personally raised funds for the building of firehouses and additions and for the purchase of ever-more-modern equipment. Hawleyville fire fighters rebuilt their fire-destroyed headquarters in 1937 on a mortgage which carried the signatures of each and every member of the company. Many Botsford volunteers mortgaged their own homes in order to raise funds for their 1951 firehouse project. In Sandy Hook, equipment was often transported to fires in the personal vehicles of volunteer fire company members.

In the early 1940s one more service vital to the welfare of citizens was given attention by town volunteers. The Rotary Club purchased the first town ambulance in 1941, and the Newtown Ambulance Association was born. Financed entirely by public contributions, the association designated John Sedor to organize a volunteer driver corps.

—Carole Telfair

Postcard of Main Street, 1910.

courtesy of *The Newtown Bee*

The Men's Literary and Social Club of Newtown Street

"The Men's Club," as it is better known, was founded in Newtown in 1894. Membership was limited to 20 active members, men drawn from all professions and all sections of town. The group still flourishes and has had great influence in public issues and projects.

A volume containing eight years of minutes (from 1912 until 1920) was beautifully scribed and meticulously kept by Secretary H. N. Tiemann. In its pages, there are records about the club-sponsored raising of a new central flag pole in 1914, heated arguments about school consolidation in 1918, and summaries of nearly a decade's worth of monthly meetings which always included dinner and an essay.

In his turn, each member would serve as host and as essayist, delivering a program himself or inviting a guest speaker. Although "Social" it certainly was (although confined to men), "Literary" the club was not, strictly speaking. Only one or two essayists are described as addressing literary topics.

Typical of presentations was a September, 1913 address by E.D. Briscoe, who spoke of his Civil War experiences. The secretary, Mr. Tiemann, reported, "He told of his capture while convoying supplies to Sherman, who was then on his famous march 'From Atlanta to the Sea' and the appalling conditions of the Southern prisons. He was finally 'exchanged,' so ill that the doctors refused his plea to be allowed to go home, but he persisted and got there alive but so emaciated that his own mother did not, at first, know him."

From accounts of adventures (for example, an escape from St. Petersburg at the outbreak of World War I) to apologies for prohibition to advances in dental hygiene, the topics of concern to the Men's Social and Literary Club of Newtown Street reflected a hunger for knowledge and progress. The men of this club are part of a legacy of eager civic involvement in Newtown.

The Liberty Pole

The most well-known landmark in Newtown is unquestionably the towering flagpole that stands directly in the center of the intersection of two Connecticut highways, Route 6 (Church Hill Road) and Route 25 (Main Street).

Newtown's first "liberty pole," as it was then called, was erected to celebrate the national centennial on July 4, 1876. Forty-three Newtown citizens organized and raised the necessary

rendered the garden impractical and occasionally dangerous. The lovely tradition was replaced by what has been a confusing variety of traffic signs, warnings, and arrows.

The patriotic landmark has also been the subject of great controversy. Despite complaints from highway authorities that it constitutes everything from a "traffic obstruction" to a "traffic hazard," Newtown has remained stubbornly

Raising the Pole.

photograph courtesy
The Men's Literary and Social Club of Newtown Street

$107.50 for the purchase of pole and flag.

How long the original pole stood guard is unknown, but a second one was raised and replaced by a third wooden flagpole on July 4, 1914. On this occasion, plans, funds and work crews were provided by The Men's Literary and Social Club of Newtown Street.

Surrounding the base of the landmark for many years was a flower garden protected by a low railing. The 20th century growth in automobile traffic and the paving (in 1928) of Route 25

dedicated to its flagpole tradition.

A steel version 100 feet tall was erected in January, 1950. Flags that normally fly from its peak measure 12 by 18 feet. In the mid-1980s, a giant old glory spanning 20 by 30 feet replaced the smaller flag annually from Memorial Day until Labor Day.

Maintenance of the pole and the purchase of flags have been strictly the result of donations. At various times, local businesses, civic organizations, and private individuals have all contri-

buted to the cause of Newtown's flagpole. During the 1980s , the liberty pole gained a valuable friend in Lieutenant David Lydem of the Newtown Police Department. Taking a special interest in its history and welfare, Lt. Lydem volunteered in 1983 to help raise funds for the replacement of a gold leaf ball at the top of the pole. His efforts were successful, and he eventually inherited the job of chief Newtown flagpole expert and seeker of donations for occasional upkeep, painting, and the purchase of new flags.

photograph courtesy of *The Newtown Bee*

Religion in the 20th Century: Increased Diversity

In the early history of Newtown, as in nearly every New England town, religion was very little separated from the community's political and social life. Up until the 1950s Newtown was served by the Congregational Church, Trinity Episcopal Church, St. John's Episcopal Church, Newtown United Methodist Church, St. Rose of Lima Roman Catholic Church, and Congregation Adath Israel, established by 12 Jewish families in 1909.

There was considerable growth and expansion, however, in the religious organizations of Newtown during the 1960s and then again during the 1980s. Reasons were multifaceted, but there was above all a manifestation of a diverse people moving into what had up until that time been a predominantly rural community.

The decade of the 1960s, throughout the country, was marked by a turning away from the traditional, while at the same time reaching out in a very traditional way to satisfy spiritual needs. It was a time of growth for some religious organizations; a time when home missionaries or "planters" started new churches in communities surrounding long-established urban churches, often beginning with meetings in the homes of members.

One manifestation of the religious growth that accompanied population growth in the area is the Newtown Christian Church. Distinguished by a large, back-lit wooden cross on one side and an interior "church-in-the-round" arrangement, the building was constructed in 1969 at the intersection of Rock Ridge Road and Route 302.

The Newtown Christian Church began as the Newtown Church of Christ, initiated by the Go Ye Chapel Mission based in New York. The group met in Edmond Town Hall until land was purchased "for the consideration of $1" from Clifford Hansen of Brooklin, Maine, in 1968. The first pastor was Gerald Dye from Pennsylvania.

The fundamentalist movement of the 60s also spawned the Bible Baptist Church. Located on Sugar Street, the church was organized when Newtown families, members of the Baptist Church of Danbury, began meeting in private homes. The meetings took official form in 1963 when Ronald and Marion Bantle came from New York State to serve the foundling organization and to plant a new church. Services were held at the Newtown Middle School and in the Bantle home until 1966, when members purchased five acres of former farmland and built the facility to accommodate 250 people. In 1968 a church parsonage was added.

Above, The Dove of Peace weathervane adorns the steeple of the Newtown Congregational Church on the corner of West Street and Castle Hill Road.
photograph by Robert Klein

Right, view from the top of Castle Hill.
photograph courtesy of *The Newtown Bee*

Above and below,
The Newtown Congregational Church, West Street.

photographs by Ken Kast

The growth of these two churches closely followed the emergence of the fundamentalist movement that occurred throughout America at that time. The establishment of the congregations in Newtown exemplified new residents' wishes to adhere to traditions that were important to fundamentalists rather than being assimilated by the already-established religious organizations.

Lutherans, too, treasured the traditions of their denomination. As they moved to Newtown from other parts of the country, away from family and things of geographic familiarity, several turned to traditional Lutheran worship as a way to keep their identity.

The Reverend Mr. James Ilten and his wife were sent to explore the possibility of establishing a mission church in Newtown. He spent several months in 1960 going door to door, making friends with people who later became charter members of the church. The first meeting, with about 90 persons in attendance, took place at Hawley School in January of 1961 — with the thermometer dipping to 28 degrees below zero.

That frigid beginning notwithstanding, 11 months later 50 people signed a charter organizing Christ the King Lutheran Church. Services continued in Hawley School for several years until 1964 when the group built a parsonage and later the main sanctuary on donated land on Mount Pleasant Road at Tory Lane. In 1989 a 4,800 square-foot wing and expanded parking facilities were added.

During the tumultuous era of the 1960s, municipal and volunteer agencies were developed to deal with concerns of the burgeoning population — concerns which were once considered to be part of the duties of the clergy. The town's first full-time social worker and first full-time parks and recreation director were appointed during that decade. At the same time volunteer committees, manned mostly by members of various religious organizations and with church support, were founded.

A committee, with members drawn from the churches, was formed to look at the need for housing for the elderly, which eventually led to the building of Nunnawauk Meadows. F.I.S.H. and Meals on Wheels were organized to provide assistance to shut-ins; the Adventure Center, a non-profit nursery school served preschool children. The Sixty-Plus Club, an organization designed to provide for the social needs of senior citizens, and F.A.I.T.H., an ecumenical pantry set up to give temporary aid to persons suffering from a financial setback, were also organized with church support.

At the same time in the churches there was an increasing move toward an ecumenical spirit. Church Women United brought women from each of the religious organizations in Newtown together and united them with women all over the world. Children from each denomination found a welcome in the youth organizations and youth choirs of the town's churches.

During the 1960s, too, the old established Newtown churches were changing. Continued growth and devotion on the part of members of the Trinity Episcopal Church led to an addition which was dedicated on December 19, 1965.

Having added a new school and convent complex in 1957-58, St. Rose of Lima Catholic Church members, under the leadership of Monsignor Walter R. Conroy, turned their attention to the 1883 main building. Fears that it was no longer structurally sound led to a drive for a new sanctuary. Ground was broken in 1968, and the new home of St. Rose, accommodating 750 worshippers, was dedicated in 1969.

It was during this decade that Congregation Adath Israel benefited from the efforts of a second generation of persons whose forefathers had emigrated to Newtown at the turn of the century. A new building was erected on the original site over a new basement structure which allowed room for a social hall and kitchen.

During the 1980s, Rabbi John Nimon was the first ordained rabbi called to serve the group, and the synagogue elected its first woman president, Sybil Blau.

The Newtown United Methodist Church also experienced a rebirth and new growth, which led to the necessity of moving the church across Church Hill Road onto 40 acres of land purchased for the purpose. The church, originally built in 1850, was turned around so that the front door still faced the main highway and was set on its new foundation on September 15, 1972. In 1989 the church broke ground for a further building to house expanded services.

Due to a history of short-term stays by young clergymen, the church's chronicle gave credit to the steadfastness of a handful of women who kept the doors to the church open over its long history. Members of the Dorcas Society raised money to pay church bills by making and selling quilts, holding fairs, food sales and auctions, and selling (even delivering) lunches to men working in nearby factories during the decades following the depression.

St. John's Episcopal Church in Sandy Hook also experienced new growth in the 1960s, and in this church, as well, women have played an important role in the day-to-day operation.

In 1982, St. John's parish welcomed Joan Horwitt, Newtown's first female priest. She brought new growth to the congregation and took a special interest in F.A.I.T.H. Her efforts were instrumental in establishing the annual town-wide interfaith Thanksgiving dinner started in 1988.

Church members recall a story about a child in the congregation who wanted to

Top, St. Rose of Lima Roman Catholic Church, Church Hill Road.
Bottom, The Newtown Church of Jesus Christ of Latter-Day Saints, Saw Mill Road.

107

above, photograph by Ken Kast
below, photograph by Elliott Henry

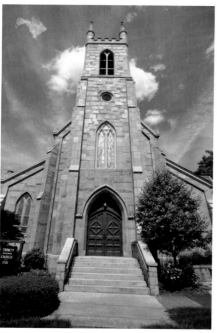

know where the "real" priest was when Ms. Horwitt was replaced during her vacation by a male priest. Evidently the mother had a hard time convincing her that a priest could be *male*!

Three more new denominations were established in Newtown during the 1980s, and one of the oldest congregations in the town's history found a new home.

Grace Christian Fellowship was founded by Barry and Sheila Fredericks on June 17, 1984. The church began with nine members and had grown to 200 within five years.

In the beginning, the group rented the banquet hall of the Essex House on Route 6 for Sunday morning and evening services. In 1986, the lower level of the building was renovated to house services while the congregation made plans for erecting its own building.

In 1979, construction of an edifice for the The Church of Jesus Christ of Latter-Day Saints, commonly known as the "Mormons, " was begun on Saw Mill Road. The church was dedicated in the spring of 1981.

Worship had been held in various places in the area for about 15 years while building-fund donations were accumulated. One very interesting fund raiser was the making of a ton of "Famous Mormon Fudge" to be sold each year at The Great Danbury State Fair. During 10 years of candy making, $50,000 was raised for the new church.

There were 200 members at the time of the sanctuary dedication, a quadrupling of charter numbers. By the late 1980s, the Newtown Church of Jesus Christ of Latter-Day Saints had 900 members.

On June 19, 1988, members of the Newtown Congregational Church had their first service in a new home on West Street on 10 acres of land that had been given to them by the Nettleton family 20 years before.

Services began in the old Main Street church, built in 1810. This structure had also served as the governmental seat for the town in its infancy. When plans were made to build anew, the Congregationalists set up an Old Sanctuary Committee charged with finding a way to preserve one of the town's most famous landmarks.

The church council voted to turn the building over to the town, but it wasn't until the Heritage Preservation Trust of Newtown, Inc., was formed that the town accepted the building. The Trust became responsible for maintaining and preserving the old building, bringing it in line with fire and safety codes and deciding on appropriate public uses.

This action eventually provided space for the final new religious organization of the 1980s. The Community Presbyterian Church held its first services in the old Congregational Meeting House on May 7, 1989 with the Reverend Mr. William Kessler presiding. An Orthodox Presbyterian Church, the 30 members had been meeting in a Danbury school for two years. Services began in 1981, with a small group of people meeting in homes for Bible study.

—Shirley Ferris

Left, Christ the King Lutheran Church, Mt. Pleasant Road.
photograph courtesy of *The Newtown Bee*

Preceding page: Center, Newtown United Methodist Church, Church Hill Road; top left, St. John's Episcopal Church, Washington Street, Sandy Hook; below left, Trinity Episcopal Church, Main Street.
photographs by Ken Kast

Planting A New Culture While Tilling the Land

The story of the Jewish men who came to Newtown at the turn of the century searching for a new home for their families is not unlike that of other peoples emigrating to the area from European countries. But the Jewish heritage and culture indigenous to the families that developed farms in the Huntingtown Road area created a special community.

The early families included the Buskers, Goosmans, Nezveskys, Epsteins, Steinfelds and the Bernsteins. Several of the descendants of these original families still live in the area and recently they got together to record an oral history of the community.

The history reveals that the lives of the children revolved around religious services, farm chores and the one-room schoolhouse. Most of the students at the school were Jewish as there were only three Gentile families in the area so the rabbi would call up school superintendent Carl LeGrow at the beginning of the year and tell him when the Jewish Holidays would be for the upcoming year and the school would be closed on those days.

But that didn't mean Christian customs were ignored. Indeed, Christmas traditions were followed, right to a "T," according to Sylvia Nezvesky Kirschblum, who said that while Jewish children weren't allowed to have Christmas trees in their homes they made chains out of colored paper and decorated trees in the woods.

And the Jewish families were cognizant of other aspects of the larger community they shared with townspeople: "You graduated from the one-room school," according to Sam Stern, "when you were able to read *The Bee*."

There was no transportation to Hawley School from Huntingtown. Often children would be able to get a ride to school in the morning but usually had to walk the six miles home.

Ethel Miller Freedman, who coordinated the oral history, taught Sunday School to the children of these families some 50 years ago.

photograph by Ken Kast

"I remember taking the Danbury-Bridgeport bus and meeting the farmers," Mrs. Freedman said, recalling two seasons she taught in Huntingtown under the auspices of the Council of Jewish Women in New York City.

The farmers took turns picking her up at the general store, at the crossroads of Huntingtown and Meadowbrook Road and took her to the synagogue. The boys took turns bringing in wood and lighting the potbellied stove early in the morning before her arrival. . . .

Farm Chores

Daily living on these farms was no easy task and youngsters would rise early to do chores with their fathers before going off to school. After school they fed and watered the cattle and cleaned chicken coops and barns.

Thursday was market day for the farmers of the Huntingtown community. This was the day that produce such as cheese, cream, eggs, vegetables, and chickens were piled into horse drawn wagons and carted to Pembroke Street in Bridgeport.

The milk collected from the farms had to be taken to the main road, three or four miles away, to be picked up by the Borden Dairy or Mutual Farm Dairy which was owned by Henry and Samuel Belinkie.

In the winter, with snow on the ground, the milk was transported by sled. There were no snow plows so a man named Keating, one of the non-Jewish residents of Huntingtown plowed the road and the town reimbursed Mr. Keating for his work.

Community History

Baron Maurice de Hirsch, the grandson of the first Jewish landowner in Bavaria, was enormously wealthy and in 1831 he established the Baron de Hirsch fund for the benefit of Jewish immigrants. The activities of the trust included helping displaced Jewish families, through loans, settle in rural areas in the United States.

Jacob Goosman came to Newtown via the Hebrew-Immigrant Aid Society which was funded by the baron. Jacob was a carpenter who arrived in Newtown in 1909, after spending three years in New York City. Before long Jacob, his parents and wife Sophie, brother Shia (Sam) and sister Fannie Gitovitz and her husband all owned farms on Huntingtown Road.

Following what appears to be a pattern of the lifestyles of even the very earliest farming settlers in Newtown, Jacob and Shia also had jobs off the farm. The Goosman men worked in Bridgeport, Jacob as an automobile painter for Ryan and Litz on Colorado Avenue and Shia as a presser for the Levine Coat Company. . . .

Jacob also took advantage of another source of income for the farmers of the area. He built a second home next to his original dwelling for summer resident use.

Besides extra revenue for the farmers, the practice also brought new excitement to the neighborhood, especially when it led to the building of establishments like the Sunrise Hotel.

In nearby Botsford, a railroad stop in those days, Eli Goldblatt operated the Sunrise Hotel (where Ashlar is located today). There were Saturday night dances on summer nights that were attended by local young men and women and summer residents from New York. . . .

Two of Jacob Goosman's children, Fannie and Thomas, still reside in the Newtown area. Tom Goosman, formerly a member of the Board of Selectmen, is well-known to Newtown residents for more than 42 years of service to the town with the volunteer ambulance corps. Tom and his wife Lily and daughter Lisa live on Meadowbrook Road and Sherman Goosman, his son, lives in Sandy Hook.

Another resident whose face is familiar to many Newtown residents is Aaron Bernstein, a school bus driver. His wife, Doris, is a home economics teacher at the high school. His grandfather, Wolfe Bernstein, bought the farm on the corner of Meadowbrook and Huntingtown Roads and the house was eventually passed on to Aaron's son Ben. . . .

No story is complete without a romance and the Huntingtown saga is no exception. Isadore Kaufman was brought from Russia to live with his uncle, Harry Schopick. Isadore had no

interest in farming and began a career buying and selling cattle.

One summer day he was driving through Stepney, according to the oral history, calling on farmers when he met a young lady named Minnie who was the governess for a summer boarding family. The two were married and

Ground breaking for the synagogue, July 4, 1914.

photograph courtesy of Samuel Nezvesky

Isadore bought a house and farm located between the general store and the Adath Israel Synagogue. He became very successful, according to the history, and always dressed neatly with a shirt and tie and polished shoes. . . .

The Synagogue

Charles and David Nezvesky left Mariupal, Russia in 1900. At Ellis Island their names were changed to Charles Epstein and David Epstein. Charles stayed in New York and David joined relatives in Huntingtown. Charles wrote his father, Israel, of his American life and the older man sold all the family possessions for 25,000 Russian rubles and in 1904, at age 68, traveled

with his wife and five children on the steamship "Fatherland." With the help of family and Jewish organizations, he purchased a farm in 1905 on Huntingtown Road.

Jacob and Sophie Goosman's home had a large dining area and it had been used for Sabbath and Holiday Services when the community was in its infancy. Then about 1909 Israel and Rose Nezvesky allocated a piece of land to build a synagogue and an organization of 12 Jewish families began to raise funds for the building. Many of the Jewish families around the Huntingtown district helped to dig the foundation, hauling fieldstones for the walls of the foundation over the next few years.

The actual groundbreaking for the synagogue was July 4, 1914. The cornerstone was laid in July 1919 and Adath Israel Synagogue was dedicated in 1920. Sam Nezvesky, Israel's grandson, still lives on Huntingtown Road. . . .

In 1960, through the efforts of the second generation, the building was moved, a new basement structure was built on the original site and the original building was placed on the new foundation. The new basement became the social hall with a kitchen for social events and a classroom. Improvements have been made to the interior over the years and today the building is the religious home for 100 families with 45 students attending the Hebrew school classes.

—Shirley Ferris

reprinted with permission from *The Newtown Bee*

NEWTOWN REMEMBERS
WITH GRATEFUL PRAYERS AND
SOLEMN VOWS HER SACRED DEAD
HER HONORED LIVING WHO
VENTURED ALL UNTO DEATH
THAT WE MIGHT LIVE A REPUBLIC
WITH INDEPENDENCE A NATION
WITH UNION FOREVER A WORLD
WITH RIGHTEOUSNESS
AND PEACE FOR ALL

factory who were watching, seized his hat and kept it going up in the air for quite some minutes."

Over in Taunton, Fred Luf "went out in the dark to milk and heard some queer noises up the road. There soon hove into sight a little procession headed by Grandma Olmstead, 80 years old, Miss Jennie Honan, the teacher, Mrs. Michael Honan, and many others. They had marched down Briscoe Street and were celebrating in right royal fashion. Such a day the town had never seen." Bonfires blazed on Main Street, the Sandy Hook Band played, business was suspended, and the entire town gave itself over to rejoicing.

A week later the *Bee* carried the news that PFC Carl Staler was dead in France. Like Sgt. Peck, he died of pneumonia, which, together with the influenza virus and typhus, took more American lives than did German bullets.

World War II

If a naive innocence was the trademark of Newtown's perception of World War I, the years from 1942 to 1945 were darker and more frightening. Although the town population barely topped 4,000, there were over 400 men and women from Newtown who had served in the armed forces by the time the war ended, and the costs were painful:

Captain Peter Lawson was listed as Newtown's first war fatality when his plane was shot down over the Pacific in 1942. After his death, his wife Toni left for Hawaii to work for the Red Cross.

Captain Joseph McCarthy of Main Street, who had been cited as a brilliant student in civilian life, was captured on Corregidor in 1942 and died in Japanese captivity.

Captain Clough F. Gee, husband of Katherine Cole of Sandy Hook was listed as killed in action when his plane went down.

Corporal David Winspur was killed on Iwo Jima after serving 26 months in the Marines.

William Frank, only son of Mr. and Mrs. Fred

Frank of Gray's Plain, was killed in a superfortress over Japan.

Marine Sgt. Charles Dean Perry, who served with the War Dog Platoon on Bougainville, was killed "somewhere in the Pacific." Three of his brothers were also in uniform at the time.

PFC Bill Hanlon, who had been the first president of the Newtown Chapter of Future Farmers of America, was killed in Italy. Pvt. Charles Carlson, the 21 year old old son of a *Bee* staff member was killed in action in France in November, 1944.

Pvt. Archie Lawrence of Walnut Tree Hill, who had been a popular clerk at the drug store soda fountain before the war, was cited, together with his old Newtown buddies, Frank Miles and Jimmy Scanlon, for aiding in taking "an important German height on the Fifth Army front." Shortly afterwards, PFC Lawrence was killed in action in Italy. At his funeral it was recalled that he had been a clarinetist in high school, and that his ambition had been to play the Adagio movement from the Mozart Clarinet Concerto. As part of the service, George Vaughan, Hawley School music teacher, "rendered it most beautifully" according to the *Bee.*.

Ben Smith of Dodgingtown, who wrote a weekly column for the *Bee*, A YANKEE POINT OF VIEW, was celebrating the approach of VE Day when he received a telegram stating that his son, Pvt. Robert Smith, had been killed in action.

Others were seriously wounded:

Frank Miles, friend of Archie Lawrence, had been an expert mechanic before the war, but he lost several fingers on his right hand when he was wounded during the drive for Rome.

Sgt. William Ryan, the first Newtown man to be called up by the Selective Service System, was invalided out of the army with extensive burns.

John (Bud) Leibold was severely wounded at

St. Lo, in France, and spent six months recovering in an army hospital.

Private Robert Lockwood of Sandy Hook was wounded in France after D Day and sent to hospital in England. His brother Willis had been wounded in Holland, and a third brother, Harold, was with an anti-aircraft unit in Germany.

Some returned unscathed:

Staff Sgt. Donald Stickles was the first Newtowner to receive an honorable discharge. He earned that right by serving 51 months in the Army Air Corps including 24 of them overseas, and, in 34 missions as a waist gunner, he had received a Distinguished Flying Cross, five Air Medals, two battle stars and a Presidential Citation.

Tech. Sgt. Isadore Epstein of the Huntingtown district completed 35 combat missions as an engineer gunner.

Cpl. Earl Leffingwell completed 34 months overseas and was one of the few survivors of the Third Ranger Battalion, seeing action in North Africa, Sicily, Italy, Germany, and France.

photographs by Joseph I. Kugielsky
Civil War artifacts courtesy of the Cyrenius H. Booth Library Collection.

115

PFC Julius Arnold of the Huntingtown district was cited for helping bring about the surrender of 178 German soldiers in Italy. His brother Irving, who had been a cartoonist for *The Bridgeport Post* before the war, also served in Italy.

Captain George Jackson of the Berkshire District, an archaeologist with degrees from Amherst and Yale, served as an information officer with a unit in the Pacific called the "Boomerangs" which attacked enemy aircraft. In 500 missions they succeeded in destroying 267 enemy planes.

Roland Person gained fame when he parachuted to safety over France - *after* discovering, to his horror, that there was no longer anyone flying the plane. Enemy fire which had hit the plane had destroyed the radio communications, and the pilot and co-pilot had been unable to contact the crew in the rear to say that they were bailing out.

Mr. and Mrs. Leonard Shepherd received a brief postcard from their son, PFC Bill, who had been in a German prison camp. It announced: ALIVE, HEALTHY AND HEADED BACK. LIBERATED MAY 5.

Each week the *Bee* brought the War closer to home by publishing the letters of Newtowners serving overseas. In January, 1943, the Reverend Mr. Paul Cullens of the Congregational Church had asked his congregation for a year's leave so that he could go to be a chaplain. They gave him a unanimous vote of support and presented him with a purse of $275 as he left for the Army Chaplain School at Harvard. For the next three years his letters would appear at regular intervals, from North Africa and then Italy.

"I have good days and days that are pretty blue..." he wrote, but "If ever there was an opportunity for a chaplain" it was when he was stationed with 2400 wounded and convalescing soldiers, and "A little bird told me there were supplies available..." Mr. Cullens commandeered a captured German truck and drove to the supply depot at the dock, circumvented the usual red tape, and came back with all manner of loot for his patients, including 1,000 new books for them to read.

Lieutenant Eleanor Jones, daughter of Dr. and Mrs. Will Jones of Main Street, wrote of doing hospital work in France where they performed "hundreds of operations a day," but feeling safer than in England "where the pilotless planes are raining on London."

PFC Bob Gannon, who before the war had been the chief chef at Fairfield Hills Hospital, participated in the liberation of Dachau. Reflecting on that experience, he wrote that "things of this nature made me proud to be an American . . . one of the reasons it is imperative that we keep the States filled with the spirit of unity and free from discrimination and prejudice."

Lieutenant Willard Duckworth wrote to the Editor from a German Prisoner of War camp. On a cramped post card was the scrawled message:

DEAR PAUL....

INTROSPECTION WORST ENEMY HERE. MANY SUCCUMB. THE OTHERS FORCE SELVES TO KEEP BUSY. MANY LEARNING TO PAINT AND DRAW. RESULTS REMARKABLE. ONE OFFICER BUILT A 12 ROOM MANSION TO SCALE OUT OF CARD-BOARD. ANOTHER MODELS PLANES FROM WOOD SCRAPS. ACADEMIC COURSES TAUGHT FROM LIMITED AMOUNT OF TEXTBOOKS, MOSTLY FROM MEMORY. MAIL IS RATHER ERRATIC. WE NEVER LOOK BACK. ONLY AHEAD TO TOMORROW. BY-WORD- 'KEEP BUSY-THIS CAN'T LAST FOREVER.'
YOURS, DUCKWORTH

On the home front, the threat, the cost, and the resolve to fight the war unified the town and brought together people of all ages and backgrounds. Many participated in the Home Guard and other Civilian Defense projects:

In October, 1942, the Newtown Motor Corps was organized and a motor mechanics course was given by Louie Lovell at Lovell's Garage. Six members completed the 14-hour course, and Miss Sarah C. Farrell (who would become Mrs. William Mannix in 1945) was named Captain.

In 1943, an aircraft spotting post was opened on Mount Pleasant, to be staffed by local volunteers and thereby relieve military personnel for other duties. Harrie Wood, a Newtown artist, was the chief observer, having taken the Army's Aircraft Recognition Course in New York City. Wood arranged with high school principal Carl LeGrow to set up a regular class in which Wood could train student observers.

Each week volunteers would meet to roll bandages for military hospitals. The town had a quota of 2000 surgical dressings per week, and this was the one area where Newtowners were not forthcoming. Red Cross Chairman Judge Paul Kavanaugh would call for volunteers, perennially lamenting that the previous week's turnout was not large enough. Right before D Day, Kavanough announced that, with 329 boys in the service, it was a shame that only 16 relatives turned up to work. "It is just possible that the public spirited men and women of Newtown are not truly cognizant of the great need. . ." he complained. The following week he turned to the high school for volunteers, and found a much larger supply.

Financially the townspeople were very generous with their contributions, even though they were barely out of the Depression. Quota systems had been established for every community for Liberty Loans and the Red Cross. Newtown surpassed its quotas regularly, and in 1944 was awarded a prize - a captured German helmet contributed by the War Department - for being one of the first 100 towns to meet its War Bond quota of $493,000.

Children were encouraged to donate their

pennies. The Camp Fire membership voted unanimously to contribute their weekly dues of ten cents.

In March, l944, according to the *Bee*, "four little girls aged 7-10 put on a most successful circus" in the Berkshire district. The show included pageants, acrobatics, and animal acts featuring the Janes' pet goat as star performer. Children from Sandy Hook school were bused over to see the circus and candy and cookies were sold, raising a net profit of $12 for the Red Cross.

Hawley School made a tremendous effort to involve the children. The entire school devoted ten minutes of every day to fund raising through the sale of War Stamps (which were in much cheaper denominations than War Bonds), and Mrs. Charles Goodsell of the mathematics department prepared a graph to keep track of their progress. As a group they raised $3350, enough to pay for two army jeeps, and by June, 1944, they received the right to fly the Minute Man flag, in recognition of the fact that 92.5% of the students were buying stamps regularly.

The films playing at the Edmond Town Hall movie theater reflected the mood of anxiety mixed with patriotic determination - each week the folks at home could go to see stars like Spencer Tracy in *The Seventh Cross*, Dana Andrews in *A Wing and A Prayer*, Irene Dunne in *The White Cliffs of Dover*. For comic relief there were lighter offerings such as *This is the Army, See Here Private Hargreave*, and *Four Jills In A Jeep*.

Always, there was the prevailing sense of shortages of *everything*, and the need to scrape and save and make do, so that vital supplies could go to The War.

The Parker House joked in its ads: "OUR

MEALS ARE AN APPETIZING RELIEF TO ALL WHO ARE BOTHERED WITH FOOD SHORTAGES!" and, towards the end of 1944: "DO YOU LIKE TO EAT GOOD FOOD? AS LONG AS OUR POINTS HOLD OUT   [we will serve it]!"

To supplement wartime diets affected by the rationing coupons that limited the amounts of meat, sugar, milk, and butter to be had, people planted Victory Gardens. In 1944, 97 families were officially registered as keeping these

Troops training at Castle Ronald during World War I.   photograph courtesy of Kenneth L. Peck

gardens and the Victory Canning Corps produced 10,648 quarts of canned fruits and vegetables, 49 quarts of soup, 1,916 jars of jellies and jams, and 547 jars of pickles.

Because of the war in the Pacific, rubber was in such short supply that obtaining a new set of tires was newsworthy enough to get your name printed in the paper. Vehicles were kept going with retreads and patches, as typified by the ad placed by a New Milford Dealer: "ATTENTION FARMERS; WE ARE IN A POSITION TO VULCANIZE YOUR TRACTOR TIRES AND

TUBES AND REPLACE OLD TRACTOR TUBE VALVES!"

Each month the Boy Scouts, Girl Scouts, and Camp Fire Girls helped in the collection of scrap metals and fat. A typical month's take included 947 pounds of fat, which was held in barrels at various food stores until it could be shipped off to be used in making soap and other items, and 6,370 pounds of various kinds of metal.

By the D Day Invasion, the drive was expanded to include all kinds of scrap paper. Since the wood supply from Scandinavia was cut off, there were serious paper shortages. Not only was paper needed for normal peacetime purposes, but it was also necessary for containers, bomb bands, parachute flares, wingtips, and airplane signals.

The phone company placed huge ads urging people to "GIVE SEVEN TO TEN TO THE SERVICE MEN - HELP HIM GET THAT LONG DISTANCE CALL THROUGH TONIGHT. YOU CAN DO IT BY NOT USING LONG DISTANCE BETWEEN 7 AND 10 P.M. EXCEPT FOR URGENT CALLS. THOSE ARE THE NIGHT TIME HOURS WHEN MANY SERVICE MEN ARE OFF DUTY AND IT'S THEIR BEST CHANCE TO CALL HOME."

As the tide began to turn and the American Invasion armies slowly fought their way through France and Italy, attention began to focus on the desperate plight of civilian refugees in wartorn Europe.

Newtowners were urged to leave bundles of clothing at the Congregational Church for people in 44 United Nations countries currently living in "clothes we would not even handle." The Rotary

Club collected money for the children of bombed out London.

Newtown had its own personal "refugees" in Charles Luyens and Albert van Ackelyen, two Belgian boys living in exile in England. In July, 1944 a series of five square dances were held to raise money for Charles and Albert, whose letters of gratitude were published in the newspaper, and the organizers were delighted with the $120 collected, which was enough to support the pair until March, 1945.

Ridgefield set up a permanent depot for Russian War Relief to provide supplies from the area for newly liberated Russians. For a cost of $2.75, a kit could be put together containing, among other necessities, sugar, soup mix, soap, bandages, gloves, knitting needles, buttons, pipe tobacco, cookies, and hard candies.

Dr. Sabine Gova, a Belgian physician who had spent time in refugee camps, made a "stirring appeal" at the Spring Luncheon of the Newtown Women's Federation, asking guests to urge the government to cut red tape and feed the children of Europe. Against the background of "a perfect spring day" with "charming arrangements of dogwood and apple blossoms" she described "the ugliness and cruelty of the daily lot in Europe." Food was ready and waiting, she said, neutral countries would provide ships, and the International Red Cross would ensure that German troops got none of it. She called for pressure on labor leaders and churches of all faiths to begin making a better world.

—Julie Stern

F. A. Stoddard and H. N. Tiemann pack books at Booth Library for a W. W. II Victory Book campaign. Photograph published in the February 27, 1942 *Newtown Bee*.

Castle Ronald

Once upon a time there was a castle on a hill in Newtown, and the lives of those involved in its nearly 60 years of history read like a fairy tale.

Peter Lorillard Ronald, a New York based world traveler and millionaire, selected 53 acres on the sight that would later be known as "Castle Hill" in 1888. An eccentric and flamboyant character, Ronald then set out to construct a building unlike any other in the country — "more of a castle than a house."

Two thousand tons of granite and cut stone were lugged up the hill to form walls two feet thick. Flanked by two long wings, a central section 110 feet long featured a drive-through carriageway. From wine cellars to servants' quarters to a gymnasium and Turkish and Russian style baths, the end product lived up to the owner's lavish tastes. A conservatory on top of the central wing provided strawberries, fig trees, and a view of Long Island Sound.

An anxious town awaited the arrival of the owner and his family. To the surprise of all and the consternation of not a few, Mr. Ronald installed not his wife, the former Mary Frances Carter of Boston, in his fabulous castle, but his "secretary" and alleged mistress, Miss Elizabeth Blake. Townspeople regretted that they would never meet Mrs. Ronald, who had been welcomed at the British Court by Queen Victoria. What they did not suspect was that the socialite Mary Frances Carter Ronald was rumored to have had a less august relationship with some of the brightest masculine stars of her day.

When Peter Lorillard Ronald died in 1905, he left to his mistress the castle, but not the means to support and maintain it. Despite her and later owners' attempts to establish various profitable institutions of treatment and education in the castle, financial resources were always inadequate, and the building was finally demolished in 1947.

The Arts in Newtown: Notes and Profiles

The history of the fine and performing arts in Newtown is as colorful and unique as the history of the town itself. It has been called "home" by many of those distinguished in the fields of painting, sculpture, literature, music, and theater. Newtown has also played host to many renowned, talented guest artists.

Arts Organizations

The Newtown art sector has been well represented through various town organizations. These groups may indeed represent only a partial picture of the many-faceted artscape of Newtown, but they offer a glimpse of the rich artistic resources of this community.

Musical Notes

It was in the winter of 1932 that the minister of the Newtown Congregational Church, Paul Cullens, formed a group called the "Tinkerfield Players," which consisted of seven musicians interested in occasional performance and ensemble playing. Their colorful name had been taken from the south center district of town which at one time had been known as Tinkerfield. After a year of performances given at local church suppers and Fairfield State Hospital, the group increased from the original seven to 41 amateur and professional musicians. They changed their name and became the Newtown Orchestra. By 1946, when they presented a series of concerts, the symphony orchestra numbered 55 members. The Newtown Orchestra presented their last concert in August, 1948.

In 1970, an ambitious, music loving group of Newtowners incorporated the Newtown Arts Festival. Their goal was to bring high caliber professional entertainers to Newtown. Their novel idea was met with much enthusiasm and their advance subscription tickets for performances at the recently-built Newtown High School guaranteed success. Performers such as Marilyn Horne and the New Jersey Symphony Orchestra as well as dancers from the Bolshoi Ballet, the Vienna Choir Boys, and the Benny Goodman Sextet performed in Newtown.

Though the entertainment was superb, conditions at the 1200 seat capacity high school auditorium were not. Problems of heating and ventilation, acoustics, and stage limitations plagued the organization. By the ninth year subscription tickets drastically dropped, and this multi-arts presentation plan was abandoned.

In 1977, a group of classical music lovers drew up by-laws and incorporated as a

From 1970 to 1979 the Newtown Arts Festival sponsored a variety of performers and performances in town. This photo collage by Ellen Fahrenholz represents some of the groups and soloists who enriched Newtown's art scene under the auspices of the Festival.

non-profit organization known as the Newtown Friends of Music. The philosophy of the organization was recorded in the minutes of their preorganizational meeting on October 24, 1977. It reads: "We believe that there should be a setting in Newtown for families and individuals to hear live musical performances . . . Our intent is to emphasize classical music representing all musical periods. In addition, we hope to provide younger professionals and area musicians with a performance setting."

Town Players

In May 1937, the Reverend Mr. Paul Cullens and the Congregational Youth Group presented a two-day street fair with melodramas at the town hall. The performances were well received and inspired an organizational meeting in June of 1937, with Mr. Cullens and the Reverend Mr. William Wright of Trinity Episcopal Church presiding. Sixty Newtown residents attended this meeting, which resulted in the founding of the Town Players. In the fall of 1937, this group began production of full-length plays at the town hall.

In June 1951, Hazel and Harold Smith, members of the Town Players gave 1.3 acres of land located on Orchard Hill Road (formerly Dingly Dell Goat Farm) to the group of dedicated thespians. Up to this point, the group built sets and props at various locations and transported everything back and forth to the town hall. Storage of supplies and props became more and more of a problem. With the gift of the building site, the Town Players began constructing a cinder block storage barn which doubled as a rehearsal hall.

The last Town Players production to be given at Edmond Town Hall was in 1956. That play was "You Can't Take It With You," but ironically the Town Players did just that! They took their props, sets, and costumes with them to the Orchard Hill Road site and began using their building as the "Little Theater." Chris Sidenius, who later opened his own innovative theater of lights, *Lumnia*, installed the first lighting system for the theater.

Although the theater offered much in the field of dramatic presentations, it lacked many features of comfort. There was no running water, outdoor tents served as dressing rooms, and patrons and performers shared access to the single outhouse. In 1968, therefore, a loan was secured to build a two story addition to the existing playhouse. The group worked on a very limited budget. Tickets were only $1.50, so they depended on the generosity of patrons and kindness of strangers for support. Board members often donated monies just to get each season started.

In the 1960s and 1970s, in addition to the four play season, the theater offered summer workshops, children's theater, and initiated story hours at the library. In 1977, a foyer and indoor plumbing were added to the building.

The Town Players, the second oldest community theater in Connecticut, celebrated its 50th anniversary in 1987, at the Edmond Town Hall. Tribute was paid to the founders as well as to the many notable theater people who had aided the community theater of Newtown in offering scenes of life from all over the world on its rural country stage.

The Society of Creative Arts of Newtown

In 1970, Newtown artist Larry Newquist was teaching an oil painting class for the Adult Education program at Newtown High School when he first discussed his idea of establishing an art organization for the town. The idea was received with great enthusiasm, so Mr. Newquist initiated the first steps towards creating SCAN.

January 14, 1971, was the night scheduled for the first organizational meeting. It was also a night when nature decided to paint its own special landscape for the gathering artists. According to Mr. Newquist, "Every tree in Newtown shimmered with a sparkling coat of ice. The night air and freezing rain was really *cold*. The icy, sand-sprinkled roads defied Newtowners to venture out." Only eight people braved the weather and attended that first meeting to talk about fostering the study of art in all its facets, bringing about an exchange of views, and cooperating with other clubs in encouraging the advancement of the creative arts.

Later, the name,"The Society of Creative Arts of Newtown" was adopted, and through the years SCAN has functioned much like a bridge between community and artists.

Thanks to SCAN, and to all the artists and art organizations in Newtown, the community has indeed, seen more than a single world. The art community has extended the boundaries of Newtown to as far as the imagination can take it.

—Joanne Greco Rochman

Profiles

Andrei Hudiakoff

After a 1983 interview with artist Andrei Hudiakoff, a League of Women Voters representative wrote:

> *Andrei is an artistocratic looking, slim little old man, with his*
> *shoulders slightly bent. He has wisps of greying brown hair, but*

*his blue eyes flash. He has an old world courtesy and met us at
the end of a quarter-mile long, rocky driveway. His hand goes to
his ear periodically, because he no longer hears very well. He wears a
rough jacket and slacks.*

Andrei Hudiakoff was born in a small Russian town between Moscow and Kiev. He began to paint at an early age and was a 20 year old student at the Moscow Art School when the Russian Revolution broke out in 1917.

Mr. Hudiakoff remembered what life was like for peasants before the Revolution. Students, he recalled, expected the revolt and were required to support the change. Unable to agree with the methods of the new government, Hudiakoff emigrated, arriving in the United States in 1923. Upon landing in New York City, he met a young American named Doris who became first his English teacher and later his wife.

photograph courtesy of Liz Wilson

The Hudiakoffs bought land in the Hawleyville section of Newtown in 1934 and spent time here "for enjoyment." Later they transferred their residence permanently and set up a small and unassuming house and studio. Doris Hudiakoff died in 1976; her devoted husband mourned for her until his own death in 1985.

Andrei Hudiakoff designed garden scenery for theaters in Russia by the time he was 12. He studied in the United States at the National Academy of Design and the Tiffany Foundation. He received several honors and designed decor for some of the most prestigious hotels in New York City. He decorated the Grand Ballroom of the St. Regis Hotel, the interior of the Waldorf Astoria, and murals at the Roosevelt Hotel.

His work graces the walls and ceilings of a magnificent Greek Orthodox Church, St. John the Divine, in Monessen, Pennsylvania. Paintings for that project took the artist 12 years to complete. Some of Hudiakoff's theater set design sketches from the 1920s have sold at Sotheby's for significant amounts.

Andrei Hudiakoff's neighbors and friends in Newtown have remembered him. The rose garden at the Cyrenius H. Booth Library was dedicated in part to his memory.

The Hallocks of Newtown

The Hallocks of Newtown represent three generations of artistic contributors to the local scene. Some of the most familiar visual symbols associated with Newtown can be attributed to a talent that must certainly have been passed down in this family.

Robert Hallock was a noted graphic designer whose local motifs include the Newtown Town Seal and signs for the Ram Pasture and the Cyrenius H. Booth Library. On the national scene, he was responsible for the design of several commemorative postage stamps and for the publication of a prestigious art professionals' journal.

Robert and Marian Hallock's son John often worked with his father. In 1974, he designed and crafted the landmark "bee" weathervane atop the office of *The Newtown Bee* on Church Hill Road.

John Hallock passed his sculpture skill on to his son John. Together they conceived the design of another Newtown weathervane — this time for the relocated Newtown Congregational Church on Castle Hill Road. The old rooster remained on the original building. The Hallocks' creation was based on the dove of peace symbol, similar to a vane that graces George Washington's Mt. Vernon estate in Virginia.

Robert Raynolds: A Life in Books

A number of writers have called Newtown home. None has been more respected in his profession or more devoted to the welfare of his town than Robert Raynolds.

This prolific author was not a Newtown native; he was born in Santa Fe, where his father was serving as territorial governor. As a young man, Robert worked as a rancher in Wyoming and in the mines of several western states.

Drawing of Robert Hallock by Bernie Fuchs.
Courtesy of Marian Hallock

124

Raynolds and his wife Marguerite purchased land in Newtown in 1933. On their property stood the run down Head O' Meadow one room schoolhouse, which Mr. Raynolds repaired and renovated to serve as a private author's retreat.

Raynolds' first novel, *Brothers in the West*, won the 1931 Harper Award. Other books included *The Obsure Enemy*, *Paquita*, *The Sinner of St. Ambrose*, *The Flight of Love*, and *The Choice to Love*.

The Newtown Town Players and the plays of Robert Raynolds were a natural combination. Collaborative efforts included two well received productions in the 1937 Town Players' season: "Farewell Villain," and "Summer Song."

Dedicated both to his town and to the world of books, this well known author served as a Trustee of the Cyrenius H. Booth Library in Newtown for many years, until just before his death in 1965. The children's library on the second floor of the building was christened the Robert Raynolds Room upon its completion in 1983.

The Sleeping Visitor

Noted pianist Percy Grainger performed in Newtown in September, 1940. Recalling the event in 1983, organizer Agnes Cullens remembered that the great artist arrived at the train station but refused automobile transportation to the concert hall, insisting on traveling by bus. He appeared for a rehearsal, but was nowhere to be found as showtime approached and the hall was filling up with an expectant audience. Mrs. Cullens was selling tickets at the box office when word came that the pianist had just been located — sound asleep on top of the concert piano at stage center.

Mr. Grainger appeared in Newtown again after the end of World War II. A native of Australia, he was also a composer and collector of folk songs from England, Scandinavia, and the South Sea islands.

John Mulholland: The Wizard of Newtown

In a 1954 article for *The Newtown Bee*, Walter Trumbull described his friend: "Asking what I know about John Mulholland is like trying to get the facts concerning Merlin . . . . It isn't safe to pry too closely into the affairs of these necromancers. Not only are they apt to leave, but they are likely to make the questioner disappear."

John Mulholland was an internationally acclaimed magician who divided his residence between New York City and a farm on Dinglebrook Lane in the Hanover district of Newtown. However, as magic recognizes no boundaries and no language barriers, his audience was the world. He performed in 40 countries, staged command performances for royalty, and regularly donated his talents for charity benefits. He also performed in Newtown.

At an Edmond Town Hall appearance on April 21, 1954, children and the lucky adults who talked their way into accompanying them marveled at the amazing feats that this man could achieve in such a casual manner. Here was a traditional magician who was equally skilled at rope and card tricks, at pulling rabbits out of hats, and at making birds disappear into thin air. Two signature elements in his act were the Chinese ring illusion and several tricks in which he employed eight silver half dollars that he had used in his first professional appearance. Audiences of all ages loved him.

Mulholland evidentally had a devilish sense of humor. Friends related to the *Bee* a story concerning an annual play staged for charity by New York's Dutch Treat Club. As a member, John was asked to take part by playing the part of a waiter. Marking time until his entrance, Mr. Mulholland lit a cigarette and lounged in the hall outside the stage door. Passing down that same hall was the captain of the evening's catering crew. Seeing what he believed to be a loitering employee, the real waiter read Mr. Mulholland a lecture and demanded that he get rid of that cigarette immediately. With a casual smile, the magician waved his hand in the direction of his face, and the cigarette disappeared into thin air. A very surprised and speechless caterer was left gawking.

Besides his jokes and his performances, John Mulholland frequently lectured on the art of magic. He was the author of several books on the subject, including *Quicker than the Eye* and *Beware Familiar Spirits*, an exposé on the fraudulent practices of many mediums and fortune tellers.

On the death of Newtown's magician in 1970, *The Newtown Bee* published the following description: "Mr. Mulholland was a warm, gentle-mannered genius who seemed always to take his audience into the excitement of magic, and to be as pleasantly surprised as they when the seemingly impossible happened."

—Carole Telfair

Recreation: Sports, Leisure, and Conservation

The diversity of recreational life in Newtown has been especially evident in the 20th century. Increased leisure time and appreciation for the town's special advantages of space and rural atmosphere combined for a tradition of indoor and outdoor sports pastimes.

Parks

Dickinson Memorial Park, bounded by Elm Drive, Brushy Hill Road and Deep Brook Road, was dedicated in August 1955 to the late A. Fenn Dickinson, the town's first selectman who had died that spring. The 20-acre park was made possible by a $50,000 gift from philanthropist Bertram A. Stroock. In 1956 the pool was dug, and it became Newtown's only public swimming facility. The park and pool became so popular with out-of-towners in the 80s that the Parks and Recreation Commission decided to limit use to residents only. An elaborate addition to the park came in 1989, when the Funspace playground, funded by more than $60,000 in donations, was built by community volunteers.

Treadwell Memorial Park on Philo Curtis Road in Sandy Hook was dedicated in 1982. Formerly known as the Stefanko park, the 43-acre facility was named after Timothy B. Treadwell, a first selectman who, before he died in 1972, had envisioned another major park in town. A swimming pool was to be built, but that costly item was eliminated from the town budget throughout the 80s.

Lake Lillinonah Park, located at the end of Hanover Road, was a project begun by the Newtown Junior Chamber of Commerce (The Jaycees) in the late 50s. The three-acre park project included a much-used boat launch.

The Parks and Recreation Department

Town recreation became the responsibility of the Parks and Recreation Commission when the Town Charter went into effect in 1962. Before town programs were established, the recreation needs of Newtown's youth were served by the churches and such dedicated individuals as Wilton Lackeye, who organized the Sandy Hook Social and Athletic Club (SAC) around 1945; Coach Harold DeGroat, who promoted recreation in the schools; and Paul A. Cullens, minister of Newtown Congregational Church and lifelong supporter of youth activities.

Since its inception, the Parks and Recreation Department has managed the parks and organized recreation programs for the community, including the popular

"Funspace" at the Dickinson Town Park was funded and built by community volunteers.

photograph by Bill Brassard

Summer Day Camp, boys' and girls' basketball leagues, Teen Night gatherings, trips to Disney World and ski resorts, and special holiday events. The late Lee Davenson, a popular Parks and Rec director of the 70s, instituted many programs and helped get the Treadwell Park project going.

Organized sports in town grew considerably in the 70s and 80s — especially sports for girls — and as Newtown headed into the 1990s there was an organization promoting nearly every major sport. The Newtown Soccer Club, Little League, Pop Warner Football, Youth Softball Association, and Lacrosse Club were instituted in cooperation with Parks and Recreation, whose biggest headache was often finding enough fields for everyone to play on. At its inception in 1983, the biggest youth event in town became the Soccer Club's Memorial Day Weekend Kickoff Tournament, during which young players from more than 70 local and out-of-state teams have participated.

Sponsored as well were popular adult recreation activities, including the Newtown Men's Slo-Pitch Softball League and tennis. The Newtown Tennis Association, which has contributed to the building and upkeep of courts, was responsible for the Newtown Open and Bertram Stroock tennis tournaments. Runners participate in the five-mile Parks and Rec Rooster Run in the spring and *The Newtown Bee* 10-Kilometer Road Race in the late summer.

Small-town sports are always made possible by the work of devoted individuals, and, beginning in the the late 80s *The Newtown Bee* recognized them with its Sportsman of the Year Award. Winners included coaches from Newtown's volunteer and school sports programs.

Newtown's Soap Box racing drivers Michael Gallo and Matt Margules won at the All-American Soap Box Derby in Akron, Ohio in the 1980s.

Town Open Space

Despite considerable real estate development in Newtown much open space has always remained in state-, town-, and privately-owned lands. Most state-owned land has been available for use by residents. Paugussett State Forest, consisting of north and south sections, totals nearly 2, 000 acres. Paugussett North borders Lake Lillinonah and includes the Pond Brook Boat Launch, and Paugussett South borders Lake Zoar. These heavily wooded areas became popular with hikers, birdwatchers, and hunters. The 41 acre Rocky Glen State Park is a rugged area opposite Glen Road in Sandy Hook.

In 1989 the Newtown Forest Association owned 49 tracts of land aggregating 700

Harold DeGroat

photograph courtesy of *The Newtown Bee*

Newtown High School Sports

The high school sports program in Newtown has had a storied history, dating back to the days when legendary former physical education chairman Harold DeGroat arrived in 1944.

DeGroat, who was profiled in Sports Illustrated *in 1957, created a program that became the envy of the physical education profession. He helped Newtown students attain the nation's highest scores on the Kraus-Weber fitness test.*

By the late 1980s Newtown High School sponsored 19 varsity sports, often receiving state-wide acclaim. Boys' teams in football, soccer, baseball, and cross-country made several trips to state championship contests, as did NHS girls' swimming and softball teams. Coaches Peter Kohut, Pam Lupo, Deann LeBeau, and Bill Manfredonia were honored by the Connecticut Interscholastic Athletic Conference.

Individual NHS athletes have also fared well in post graduate sports activities. Steve Kordish and Mark Pottinger went on to play baseball in the minor leagues, and 1968 graduate Bruce Jenner won a gold medal in the decathlon at the 1976 Montreal Olympics.

—*Scott Benjamin*

129

acres. Its goal has been to connect many of the tracts for hiking and other passive recreation uses. The Association was developed in 1924, when Dr. Charles Howard Peck donated a gift of land — the original Town Forest on Castle Hill Road. The Association purchased in 1964 a 100-acre tract off Key Rock Road as a permanent wildlife preserve named in honor of Paul A. Cullens, Newtown activist and minister of the Congregational Church. In 1969 Anna Lord Strauss donated 95 acres adjacent to Hattertown Pond.

Town-owned open space includes Orchard Hill Preserve, 24 acres of land located between Orchard Hill Road and Huntingtown Road. Despite pressure to develop the area into ball fields, the Parks and Recreation Commission has preferred to leave it in its natural state for hikers and nature lovers.

—Bill Brassard

photograph courtesy of *The Newtown Bee*

Strong Newtown High School soccer teams have benefited from early training provided by the Newtown Soccer Club under the auspices of the Parks and Recreation Department.

Equestrians In Newtown: A Struggle With Development

Horse owners traditionally have found Newtown an attractive place to live because of its room to ride. But in the 1970s and 80s equestrians started to feel hemmed in as new subdivisions sprang up across the countryside.

The Fairfield County Hounds Hunt Club was most affected by development. For nearly half a century the Hounds had conducted their wide-ranging fox hunts in Newtown's southwest country, bordered by Route 25 on the east, Poverty Hollow Road on the west, and Dickinson Town Park on the north. The Hunt rode over its own land and through the fields of neighbors who granted rights-of-way. The fox hunters, however, found their new neighbors — people moving into new developments — to be less accommodating to the Hunt.

In 1987, the group packed its horses and hounds off to more rural Roxbury. With them went the tradition of formally dressed riders astride galloping steeds giving chase to the fox.

The Hunt had sought the rural atmosphere of Newtown in the 1930s when its original home, Westport, got too crowded. The move in 1987 from Newtown chased the Fairfield County Hounds clear out of the county for which they were named. Said a former Master of the Hunt, "Our sport is alive and well today because the former Masters were smart enough to move when they had to. I hope future members can say the same about us."

The Newtown Bridle Lanes Association, formed in 1978, grew quickly to become the representative of the horse community in town. In 1989, the NBLA formed a land trust to acquire riding easements over private land, thereby preserving riding space and linking together a trail system. The venture was designed to assure future quality of horseback riding in Newtown.

The NBLA has sponsored the biggest horse event of the year in town — the Frost on the Pumpkin Hunter Pace in October. The NBLA developed a contingent of riders for the annual

Fairfield County Hounds Huntsman Rhoda Hopkins with the foxhounds.

photograph courtesy of *The Newtown Bee*

Labor Day Parade, clinics to promote better horsemanship and a popular winter Sleigh Rally.

The Poverty Hollow Pony Club has for many years helped train the younger equestrians in Newtown. Other young riders have joined the Fairfield County 4-H horse clubs in or near Newtown.

Despite the dwindling open spaces and the departure of the Fairfield County Hounds, riding, training and raising horses have been popular pastimes in Newtown. Arabians, Morgans, Thoroughbreds, and other breeds of horses have been raised at local farms.

The only major disaster in recent equestrian history was the 1969 fire at the former Open Gate Farm. The blaze destroyed a barn but no horses were killed.

—Bill Brassard

131

Chanticleer

In the early 1980s a red hot-air balloon sporting a blue rooster on a white background frequently would take off from the Ram Pasture and float across Newtown's skies. The balloon was called Chanticleer and local balloonist Harvey Hubbell IV was at the controls.

After learning to fly in the challenging winds created by Newtown's valleys, Mr. Hubbell and Chanticleer began to travel the world. They promoted freedom, good-will, and the glory of ballooning in France, Belgium, England, and Italy. In 1984, Mr. Hubbell flew Chanticleer in Poland, becoming the first American to fly a hot-air balloon in that country. In 1981, he made a tethered flight at the President's inauguration in Washington, D. C.

"Ballooning opened up many doors," said Mr. Hubbell, who was nearly 50 years old when he took up the sport.

Mr. Hubbell said the symbol of a rooster was known everywhere he went. Modeled after the weathervane on the old Newtown Congregational Church, the Chanticleer rooster was selected by Mr. Hubbell to give the people of Newtown a sense of identification with the balloon. But he discovered that the rooster, an emblem of rural life in Newtown, had a larger significance. Many Europeans, especially the Poles, recognized the rooster as a religious symbol.

Chanticleer, constructed in England, was named after a cock in Chaucer's *Canterbury Tales*. The rooster on the balloon's side was designed to include markings representing the bullet holes that were supposedly fired into the Congregational Church's weathervane by General de Rochambeau's men. Mr. Hubbell, an enthusiast of legend and history, declared that legend full of hot air. "Rochambeau's men have taken a bum rap for many years," he said. "Local Newtown boys put the shots in. My brother fired a few. That weathervane used to spin!"

As much ambassador as balloonist, Mr.

Hubbell always draped an American flag over the side of Chanticleer's basket, even in Eastern bloc countries. "A balloon says something about freedom," he said. "You can see it up there floating free and untethered."

During one flight in Poland, Mr. Hubbell was surrounded by a large crowd after he landed; he served champagne to adults and candy to children. On another flight he landed Chanticleer in a wheat field in a village named Syberia. A farmer helped him put Chanticleer on a horse-drawn cart for a ride back to the launch site. On the way the farmer joked, "It took an American to find a Syberia in Poland."

—Bill Brassard

photograph courtesy of Harvey Hubbell

The Labor Day Parade: Newtown's Traditional Summer Finale

Balloons, bagpipes, marching bands and children from scout troops and soccer leagues and nursery schools, tiny motorcycles maneuvered by not-so-tiny Shriners — these are the sights that symbolize Newtown for many long and short term residents and for visitors from all over.

The ingredients for Newtown's Labor Day Parade were first mixed in May of 1962 at the dedication of the Dickinson Town Park. On this occasion, Stanley Verry and several other civic leaders in attendance discussed the need for some focus of pride and celebration in Newtown.

They decided to act. Labor Day weekend was perceived to be the first practical target date for the organization of a festival. Fun and togetherness were to be primary reasons for "Newtown Progress Days," but the schedule of events would also provide an excuse to keep people at home and out of dangerous holiday weekend traffic.

The first parade was accompanied by a block party and athletic events at Dickinson Park. The next year additional functions were planned, and the popularity of the weekend festivities provided incentive for the establishment of an annual tradition.

After 1967, Newtown Progress Days on the

photograph by Ted Swigart

Labor Day weekend became Newtown's Summer Festival, to be celebrated over a 10-week period each year. The Festival organizers devised a schedule of events throughout the summer, including concerts, picnics, athletic contests, and a Fourth of July celebration with fireworks, to culminate in the Labor Day Parade.

Inevitably problems did arise. After several years of explosive success, Fourth of July fireworks were dropped from the schedule due to rising insurance rates and increased difficulties in crowd, traffic, and fire control. Financial demands necessitated more and varied fund raising activities. Subscription dances (including the "Not at All Ball," which townspeople paid $5 to $10 *not* to attend), casino nights, and mail and phone appeals often rescued the Festival.

Despite budget squeaks, occasional bad weather, and even with the addition of other popular Festival activities, the Labor Day Parade continued to reign supreme as THE event of the summer in Newtown. With a different theme every year, it has become quite simply a reflection of Newtown's spirit — New England, small town, and volunteer enthusiasm all packed into one late summer's day.

133

"There is a history in all men's lives."
William Shakespeare
Henry IV, Part II

epilogue

"I don't know why you would want to talk to me about the history of New-town, except that maybe I'm one of the oldest people in town . . . by Christmas, I'll be 97 years old . . ."

—Karl Gulick

ewtown's history, like that of other towns or nations or events, is a composite. Those who attempt to record any particular version of the past draw on previously written books, diaries, journals, and newspapers as well as on the legends and stories of countless individuals. The finished work is in a very real sense simply a collection of varying opinions, perceptions, and experiences.

The real historians of Newtown are, then, her citizens. In preparing this exploration into the community's distant and recent past, we have borrowed the thoughts and memories of Newtowners throughout the years.

In company with a long list of often anonymous voices from the past, a number of contemporary townspeople have contributed to this effort. It is their memories, perceptions, and stories that appear in these pages. Their individual Newtown experiences, along with our own, are now a part of recorded history.

We recognize, however, the existence and validity of all the unpublished versions. Every person we were not able to interview has a similarly unique Newtown story. For some, Newtown is a fresh experience — perhaps a fleeting one to file with memories of many other towns. For others, this is the special place where the children grew up and were educated or where some momentous life event altered the course of a family's future. Still others have called Newtown "home" for a lifetime. Whether the memories reflect one or 80 years residence, there are literally as many Newtown histories as there are Newtown citizens. It is our regret that we could not capture in print every one of them. It is our hope that these images presented by the few will refresh and stimulate the individual memories of all Newtowners.

This is only one of the valuable lessons we have learned in researching and developing this historical account. Facts (momentous and trivial) about the past are really the least of our acquisitions. Some of the most interesting revelations have

"Newtown used to be an older town, you knew everyone then. Today people move too often . . . it was more country then , a closer community . . . life was slower . . .

"I used to live over on Washington Avenue . . . a man by the name of Birdsie Parsons lived next door and he had a little donkey. Every day, when the bus came by, it'd stop and toot its horn twice. The donkey'd lift its head then trot right up to the fence . . . the passengers always got off the bus to feed the little fellow . . ."

— Hazel Tilson

"One day, back when my children were young, their teacher asked me if I helped them with their home work because they seemed to have a good background. . . . I said no, but I did bring them books from the library that I thought related to what they were studying. She asked me if I would bring books to the classroom for the other children, too. . . the main school was Hawley School: that's where they had high school students as well . . . you know they only graduated 12 students a year back then. . . So I started bringing books for the other children in their class. . . After some time, I was offered $3,000 a year to be Newtown's first school librarian . . . I was so excited, but my husband didn't want me to take the job . . ."

—Marguerite Raynolds

"One Thanksgiving, years ago, my husband butchered one of our big pigs . . . must've weighed almost two hundred pounds. We'd had a good snowfall the night before so he put it on a sled and started to pull it over to our neighbor's. There was this steep hill, though, and the sled started to pick up speed 'til my poor husband couldn't keep up with it anymore . . . there was no way he could slow the sled down with all that dead weight . . . so he just jumped right up on top of the pig! It was the funniest sight — him just ridin' down that hill . . . sled, pig, and all . . ."

—Audrey Gaffney

138

concerned the nature of history itself.

We learned, for instance, that the tales of history tell themselves. Researchers, writers, and editors only borrow and sift. The selection of material is the most difficult task, because there are so many tales from lots of different viewpoints and geared to lots of different interests.

We have tried, therefore, to give readers of this volume as many views as possible. Formal or impromptu, fact or legend, transmitted by formerly-written histories or passed down by word of mouth from one generation to the next, the events related in this book are what we found to be the "true" history of our community.

Perhaps the hardest fact for writers of this type of book to accept is the impossibility of achieving a satisfying "end" for this story. The life of a town is a progression. A history book may halt it at one moment in time and hold it still for study. We may analyze the progress to date and make speculations about probable directions the future will take. But the flow of the progression can be held still for the moment only to the same extent that an athlete in action can be frozen in a photograph. Even during the process of holding, during the analysis and the speculation, the action continues to unfold — and things are already different.

Each new day's events add a note to history that in some way affects the whole story. So the record written yesterday is not the complete picture today. There are no clever methods to bring all the parts together into a neat resolution. The satisfaction of having the "last word" is unattainable.

This project was not, of course, undertaken with the object of drawing a new conclusion to history. The inevitability of Newtown's continued evolution and change is reassuring. Our part in recounting and evaluating the progress of history — at this particular moment in time — is done. Newtown's story, however, continues and will continue to unfold. Today's events, and those of tomorrow, we leave to future historians.

—Carole Telfair
photographs and oral histories by Linda Napier

Helen Guman and Effie Berglund

"We had the perfect life because we accepted things as they were . . . we didn't know any different. We had bread, we had butter, and we could live . . ."

—Helen Guman

.

Appendices

Historical Notes Concerning the Whos, Whats, and Wheres about Newtown

Appendix i
Highways and Byways

Many of the road and street names in Newtown have historical connotations. Street signs carrying familiar names like Baldwin, Beach, Bennett, Botsford, Peck, Glover, Scudder, etc., bring to mind the early families of Newtown. Other names have been derived from local legends or geographical features and landmarks. Some of the more familiar and more interesting examples follow.

Academy Lane was named for the Newtown Academy, which was originally built in 1937 to serve the need for education beyond the district elementary level.

Aunt Park Lane and *Phyllis Lane* pay tribute to two 19th century women who were known for the medicinal remedies they grew or found in nearby woods and fields.

Bennetts Bridge Road led to one of the earliest bridges to cross the Housatonic, connecting Newtown with the Kettletown section of Southbury. The family name Bennett was common in the town's early history.

Boggs Hill Road skirts the area referred to in the town records of 1716 as "Ye Great Boggs and Ye Little Boggs."

Borough Lane forms part of the southern boundary of Newtown borough.

Button Shop Road gets its intriguing name from one of the factories along the branches of the Pootatuck which manufactured buttons and combs from horns and hooves. In the mid 1800s Newtown had more buttonshops than any other town in the state.

Church Hill Road was originally known as the North Cross Highway. It runs from the center of Sandy Hook to the churches on Main Street, Newtown.

Dayton Street, formerly called "Under-the-Mountain Road," was renamed in 1890 as a salute to Judge Charles W. Dayton of Sandy Hook. The story goes that Judge Dayton was challenged to ride, wearing a high silk hat, on a donkey across a newly constructed iron bridge on the road. Although he chose to cross instead by means of horse and buggy, the wager was determined to have been won, and the road — as agreed — was named in his honor. The bridge has since been closed to vehicular traffic.

Goodyear Road was named for the famous inventor who discovered the process of rubber vulcanization in Sandy Hook in 1839.

Great Ring Road reflects a local legend that this was the spot where hunters (possibly Indians) formed a great ring to drive the game to the top of a hill.

Hanover Road led to Echo Vally, which was the site of the original Hanover Ford across the Housatonic River.

Halfway River forms a boundary between Newtown and Monroe and was supposedly the halfway point between colonial Stratford and Woodbury. The area was formerly called "Ragged Corner."

Hattertown was the site of several hat factories during the 19th century.

The "jangling" in *Jangling Plains Road* refers to contention or wrangling. A 1711 dispute over a parcel of land here became known as the "jangling division."

Jeremiah Road was probably named for Jeremiah Turner, the first white child born in Newtown. He was buried in Land's End Cemetery.

John Beach Road was christened for the famous minister and Tory who unsettled colonial Newtown by transferring his loyalty from the Congregational to the Anglican (or Episcopal) denomination.

Lake George Road does not run along the bank of a body of water. It was rather named for two local property owners, Thomas Lake and George Smith.

Man-made *Lake Lillinonah* was created in 1955 and named for an Indian princess who allegedly jumped to her death from Lover's Leap on the Housatonic River.

Middle Gate district was originally called "Bear Hills." After the opening of the Newtown-Bridgeport Turnpike in the 19th century, it was renamed because of its position near the middle toll gate of this highway.

Mt. Pleasant is one of several roads whose names were changed because of unpleasant associations with their orginal designations. This roadway had been known as "Slut's Hill."

The Nunnawauk of *Nunnawauk Road* and *Nunnawauk Meadows* was one of three Indians involved in the 1705 land purchase that led to Newtown's colonial settlement.

Papoose Hill Road is along a trail that was supposedly used by Indian mothers with babies (papooses) on their backs. The trail led uphill from the Hanover River valley.

Philo Curtis Road in Sandy Hook was named for a Newtown Selectman elected in 1843.

Pole Bridge Road led to a "pole" bridge across the river.

The Newtown-Danbury poorhouse was built on what is now *Poorhouse Road* in 1842 at a cost of $600.

Purdy Station Road is a disused trail to a mica mine. The road was named for a black shepherd known simply as Purdy. He cared for the victims of a smallpox epidemic which broke out in Hattertown during the 19th century.

Quanneapague was the Indian name for land that now comprises the Town of Newtown. Taunton Lake was called Quanneapague Pond.

Queen Street was christened in honor of Queen Anne, who ruled England from 1702 until 1714.

Sugar Street and *Sugar Lane* were named for the large sugar maple trees that lined the road from

Newtown to Bethel. Farmers tapped these for maple sugar and syrup. Many of the trees came down when the road was widened and paved by Connecticut in the 1920s.

Shut Road, once a through street, was closed off. What remained became known as "Shut Road."

Silver City Road derives its unlikely name from a dude ranch which once attracted horse lovers to the area.

There is a legend that the alcoholic spirits distilled on *Still Hill Road* were made into toddies nearby on what became known as *Toddy Hill Road.*

Tory Lane brings back the days of the Revolutionary War, when Newtown was (at least initially) a pro-English stronghold.

Wendover Road acquired its picturesque name in the 1940s, when residents voted by an 8-7 margin to replace "Carcass Lane." In the minds of many of the neighbors, the old title brought back upleasant recollections of a slaughterhouse previously located at the end of the passageway.

A lake, a bridge, a road, and an early school district were all called *Zoar*. In the Old Testament, Zoar was the only one of the cities of the plain to escape destruction. Lot and his daughters took refuge there.

— Pat Denlinger and Judy Furlotte

Apendix ii
Who Lived or Lives in Newtown?

Three governors of Connecticut were born or lived here. *Isaac Tousey*, elected governor in 1846, also served in the U. S. Congress and Senate. *HenryDutton* became governor of Connecticut in 1854, and *Luzon B. Morris* was elected in 1869.

Historican and teacher *Ezra Levan Johnson*, was born in Newtown in 1832.

Born here in 1870, *Dr. Charles H. Peck* served as a base hospital director in France during World War I.

Famous author and cartoonist *James Thurber* was a Sandy Hook summer resident.

Mack and Virginia Lee Lathrop were founders of Newtown's Lathrop School of Dance. In their days as professional dancers, they appeared with such notables as Irene Dunne, Gloria Swanson, Bette Davis, Tommy Dorsey, Harry James, Guy Lombardo, Kate Smith, and Ed Sullivan.

Grace Moore (Mrs. Valentin Parera) was a well known opera star. She lived at Faraway Meadows in Newtown from 1937 until her death in a plane crash in Copenhagen in 1947. She sang in Newtown only once, on Memorial Day, 1938, at the unveiling of the Soldiers' and Sailors' Monument on Main Street.

Women's activist and one-time National President of the League of Women Voters, USA, *Anna Lord Strauss* lived in town and donated land for the Open Space program.

Like many artists, actor *Alexander Scourby* and his wife *Lori March* divided their residence between Newtown and New York City.

Nina Blake, a local artist, painted murals at the Tavern on the Green in New York City. She designed sets for the Town Players.

Arthur Spector, who served on the town's Planning and Zoning Commission, had been a charter player for the Boston Celtics basketball team.

Film director and author *Elia Kazan* owned a house in Sandy Hook.

Boxer *Floyd Patterson* set up a training site in Newtown in the 1950s.

Aviation pioneer and early air mail pilot *Richard Botsford* was a descendant of one of Newtown's founding families.

These and many other citizens of note have lived in and visited Newtown over the years. A list of some other talented residents of the past and present would include *Wally Cox*, who played "Mr. Peepers" on television, noted sculptor *Rhys Caparn*, witty author and critic *Louis Untermeyer*, authors *William Swanberg* and *Donald Jackson*, children's author and illustrator *Steven Kellogg*, painters *Henry Schnakenberg*, *Betty Christensen*, *David Merrill*, and *Robert Cottingham*, and composer *Vaclav Nelhybel*.

Appendix iii
The Inventions and Products of Newtown

The rubber-lined linen hose was invented in Newtown by Isaac B. Harris.

In 1919, a two way tractor plow was invented by Arthur Reynolds.

In 1931, Edward B. Allen invented a work clamp for the Singer Sewing Machine.

Dr. Henry Rogers developed an optics camera in 1947.

In 1948, James Brunot shared in the development of the game of "Scrabble."

A "kabob" skewer for cooking over the fireplace was devised here in 1948.

The Pat Boone wall lamp was manufactured in Hawleyville in 1958.

Newtown resident R. E. Fulton, Jr. invented a sky hook for use by the U. S. Navy in 1960.

The Heise gauge was developed in 1965 at the Otto Heise Company on Route 25.

A cooler used by astronauts was invented in Newtown in 1969.

Benefactors

George C. Anderheggen, M. Div., Ph.D.
Newtown Counseling Center
54 Flat Swamp Road   Tel. 203-426-3021

Anonymous

John N. Aragones, M. D.
Madeline Aragones, R. N.
James, John, & Jonathan Aragones

Bartlett Tree Experts
Danbury, Connecticut

In memory of our son and brother, Joseph.
We will always love you.
Nicholas, Barbara & Nicole Borrello

Compleat Picture
Newtown, Connecticut

Compliments of
Curtis Packaging Corporation
Rt. 34, Sandy Hook, Connecticut 06482

Denlinger, Smith & Previdi, Attorneys at Law
Sutherland W. G. Denlinger, Helen Joy Previdi
In Memory of Earle W. Smith, 1905-1989

Frank and Barbara Dunn
Sarah Marsh and Anne

Shirley A. & Robert A. Frederick
Leslie & Charlie, Celeste & Bob
Austin Robert & Stephanie Lauren

Gallerie Van-OS, Fine Art & Framing
103 South Main Street

Bill and Carolyn Greene
Alex and Julie

In Memory of B. Jean Gretsch, M. D.
Member, Newtown LWV

Dr. & Mrs. Robert S. Grossman
John & Gail Grossman, Melissa & Lisa
David Grossman, Amy B. Grossman

Mr. & Mrs. William L. Hard
16 Russett Road, Sandy Hook, CT 06482

Jott & Phryttr Word & Data Services
Phyllis & Jim Hodsdon, 9 Fox Run Lane
Newtown, CT 06470 Tel. 203-426-5751

Mr. & Mrs. Louis Holzner
30 Currituck Road
Newtown, Connecticut 06470

James J. & Diana Carlisle Inman
Newtown, Connecticut

Ken Kast
Photographer

Shari Keith
Graphic Design

With deep appreciation for many happy years
spent in the old farmhouse on Gelding Brook.
from Steven and Helen Kellogg

Mr. & Mrs. Stanley Freeman King
In memory of
Frank Lemuel Johnson

Dave Kriger
Photographer

Joseph I. Kugielsky
Photographer

Sue & John Lehmann
Kurt, Craig, Karyn,
Karla & Krista Lehmann

Ed Little
Illustrator

Bob & Jane McCulloch
McCulloch Realtors
38 Church Hill Road
Newtown, Connecticut 06470
Newtown Specialists Since 1964

In memory of Pauline Mulholland
whose generous support
helped to make this book a reality.

Linda Napier
Photographer

Newtown Board of Realtors, Inc.
33 Church Hill Road
Newtown, Connecticut 06470

Newtown Savings Bank
39 Main Street
Newtown, Connecticut 06470

William A. Notaro, M.D.
Dermatology and Dermatologic Surgery
27 Hospital Avenue, Danbury CT 790-7585

Betty Lou & Jim Osborne, Bob & Inge Osborne,
Mike & Deb Osborne, Dody & Jay Cox,
 Susan & Brian White and all the grandchildren

With hearts past and present in Newtown
Les & Sue Polgar, Dave & Sara
Warren, New Jersey

David J. Rizzardi Company, Inc.
Repair Service Contractor for:
Plumbing   Heating   Well Pumps
Newtown, CT 06470

Compliments of
Meredith Ann Rizzardi
Cheryl Ann Rizzardi
David J. Rizzardi

Doug & Marjorie Rogers, with thanks to the members of the Newtown Forest Assoc. and the Newtown Town Players for their long service

Steve, Marta, Ross & Matthew Schieffer
6 Ridge Road
Newtown, Connecticut

In memory of Earle Wright Smith
Marie Roche Smith

Mr. & Mrs. R. Scudder Smith
Scott, Sherri & Matthew Scudder Baggett
David, Kim, Benjamin & Gregory Smith

Congratulations to the League for this beautiful book!   Louise & John Sylvester
Susan & Jay, Gordon, Todd & Elyse

Thank you Newtown
Doris & Mike Bornyak
Taunton Tavern, Newtown

William & Carole Telfair
Megan & Caty

Bob Tendler Real Estate
17 Church Hill Road
Newtown, Connecticut

Patrons

Compliments of:
Paul & Marilyn Alexander & Family

Anonymous

Compliments of
Centerbank

In memory of B. Stockton Meade & James Coffey
Bob & Caren Coffey, Sing & Muffy

Danbury Savings & Loan
Greater Danbury's Hometown Bank

Bill & Pat Denlinger, Jim, Julie & Diane
Carley & Harry Lee

Friend of the LWV of Newtown

Compliments of the Fuest Family
Ron, Joan, Greg & Laura

The Furlottes:
Paul, Judy, Christopher & Kevin

Henry N. Gellert D. D. S., P. C.

Gordon Fraser Gallery, Inc.
Distinctive Cards & Gifts

Since 1903 Honan Funeral Home
Wm. A. Honan, Jr., Daniel T. Honan

In memory of Mr. & Mrs. Albert Hrivnak
Huntington Road - Dairy Farm

Fly the flag high — Newtown!
Dr. and Mrs. Peter C. Jameson

John Johnson & Sons, Inc.
21 Hi-Barlow Road, Newtown, Connecticut

Ann Krane & children
Mark, Alexa, Erika Krasnickas

Keven Ann Larson & sons
Chris & Jason Barsi

We're proud to sell Newtown properties
Merrill Lynch Realty 426-4413

Newtown Color Center, Inc.
5 Queen Street, Newtown, Connecticut

Compliments of Newtown Mfg. Co., Inc.
Est. 1946 by Edwin Weber, Sr. & Hans Pietsch

Peter M. Obre, Guitarist
1 Baldwin Road, Newtown

Pitney Bowes

Rudy & Alice Ramsey
Ian, Chris & Devin

Compliments of
Rock Ridge Construction, Inc.

Robert L. Ruxin, M.D.
George H. Cohen, M. D.

In memory of Victor Sandone
Beatrice Sandone & Family

Mr. & Mrs. George E. Smallwood
Born Gessner Goodrich Hawley, Jr.

In memory of William E. Smith
Jo-Ann, Jennifer & Bill Smith

Paul S. Smith, In memory of my wife, Starr,
and my parents, Arthur & Frances Smith

Compliments of The Taunton Press

In loving memory of
Gerry & Frank Thomas

Caryl & Bill Timmel
Emily, Teddy, Rebecca & Christopher

Compliments of Julie Uris

Compliments of George & Pat Wakelee
29 Hanover Road, Newtown

Craig & Connie Weatherup

Dr. & Mrs. David Zolov
Michael, Eric, Andrew, & Jason

Friends

Mario & Gloria Abondolo
Families—Ken, Mary Starr, Milt, Stu, Phil Adams
Amaral Motors, Inc. Chrysler-Plymouth
Bruce & Cathy Andrews, Nicole, John & Jonelle

Mrs. Harold Barrett
Mr. & Mrs. Richard J. Beard
Ken, Barbara, Kathy, Doug & Steven Bigham
Gay & Tom Bogardus
Friends at The Cyrenius H. Booth Library
Mr. & Mrs. Howard F. Bowles, Jr. & Abby
David E. Brown, CPA
Sarah Michele & Kathryn Leigh Burns

Tom & Lynn Callan & Family
Mr. & Mrs. William F. Campbell
Betty & Dan Carson, Colleen, Brendan & Meghan
Lynn & Larry Christner, Allison & Jeff
Fr. James Cole, Forest Drive, Newtown, CT

Compliments of Marissa & Christina Dent
Lawrence F. Dieringer
George & Virginia Dolan & Family
Vivian, Daniel, Jessica & Gabriel Dorman

Shirley Eaton, Gary, Karen & Kristen

Gerald & Nancy Finnegan, Amy, Gerry & Diane
Merlin & Margery Fisk
Compliments of Robert & Jeanne Foege
Fuller & Durden Travel, Inc.

Gateway Bank, 30 Church Hill Road
Ellyn & Paul Gehrett

Georgia Pacific Distribution Division
Jill Giannettino, Michael E. Chop & Gizmo
Rosemarie & George Gollenberg
The Goosman Family
The Gordon Family: Laurie, Earl & Gregory

In memory of Raymond L. Hall
In memory of Robert Folger Hallock
Donald S. & Patricia M. Hammalian, Don Jr.
In memory of Terri Himes, Her Family
Judith Lin Hunt & Victoria Elizabeth Polito

Heather M. Johnson

Don & Joyce Kay, Valley View Road, Newtown
Nancy, David, Kevin & Kathryn Koonce
Compliments of Shirley & Lewis Krohn

The Lawrensons: Don, Shirley and family
The Letsons: John & Barbara, Sarah & Daniel
Peter & Susan Licht, Chris & Stephanie
John & Olive Lipusz, John Jr. , Eric, & Peter
Compliments of the Llodra Family

Burke & Violet Marshall
Compliments of Mr. & Mrs. Richard Masser
George & Carol Mattegat, Willie Mattegat
"Three Chimneys" c. 1725, The Meffert Family
Kathy & Don Mueller, Marci & Julie

In memory of Ferne C. Nawrocki
NEBODS — Western Connecticut
Thanks Newtown for everything. The Newells
Newtown Chamber of Commerce

Newtown Florist
Compliments of The Newtown Station
Newtown Women's Club
Albert H. and Marjorie W. Nichols
The Rev. and Mrs. Thomas G. Northcott

Olga, Stephen & Diana Paproski
Compliments of Richard & Frances Pitman
Mr. & Mrs. J. R. Proterra

Richard & Carol Recht
Jerry & Elaine Reidy, Maureen & Jerry, Jr.
Nelson & Jeane Roberts
Rock Ridge Country Club, Inc.
Ruffles Home   Sawmill Rd.   Circa 1779
Laurence Sabo, Nancy Brunell and Stosh
Sayles/O'Neill and CIP II Ltd Partnership
Representative Mae Schmidle
Irene & Harold Schwartz

Jim, Jeannette & Penny Talarino
Joe, Sue, Katie and Nikki Tarshis
Wallace C. & Dorothy Thomas

Louis & Julia Wasserman
John, Elizabeth, Laura and Emily Wefer
Pamela & Melvin Weill & Family
Dorothy E. Wenblad
Margaret Winchester
Richard, Janet, Kristin & Jennifer Woycik

Tom & Gail Young, Brian, Eric & Carrie

Bibliography

Andrews, Charles M., *Beginnings of Connecticut 1632-1662*, New Haven, CT: Yale University Press, 1934.

Barber, John Warner, *Connecticut Historical Collections*, New Haven, CT: Durrie and Peck, 1838.

Beach, Rebecca D., *Reverend John Beach and His Descendants*, New Haven, CT: Tuttle, Morehouse and Tayor, 1898.

Beardsley, Eben E., *The History of the Episcopal Church in Connecticut*, 2 vol., New York: Hurd and Houghton, 1865-8.

Beers, Henry, *Diary of Henry Beers* in five volumes, 1850-1870.

Berthier, Alexander, *Diary of Alexander Berthier*, Translated from the French by Mrs. Hastings Morse.

Berthier, Alexander, *Journal de la Campagne D'Amerique*, New Jersey: Princeton University Press, 1951.

Bonsal, Stephan, *When the French Were Here*, Garden City, New York: Doubleday, Doran and Co., 1945.

Boyle, John Neville, *Historical Notes and Maps, Newtown 1708-1758*, Newtown, CT: Bee Publishing Co., 1947.

Camp, Beach, *A Journal of Newtown, March 29,1831-November 18, 1832*, transcribed by Caroline Stokes.

Carlyle, Thomas, *The French Revolution*, Boston: Dana Estes Publishing Co., 1837.

Cavanaugh, Paul V., "Arthur Treat Nettleton, Newtown's First Citizen," *1950 Annual Report of the Town of Newtown*.

Cavanaugh, Paul V., "A Bit of Educational Lore," *1944 Annual Report of the Town of Newtown*.

Cavanaugh, Paul V., "A Bit of the History of Our Liberty Pole," *1948 Annual Report of the Town of Newtown*.

Cavanaugh, Paul V., "A Bit of History of Our Churches," *1945 Annual Report of the Town of Newtown*.

Coffey, Edward Nichols, *A Glimpse of Old Monroe*, Derby, CT: The Monroe Sesquicentennial Commission, 1974.

Commemorative Biographical Record of Fairfield County, CT, Chicago: J. H. Beers and Co., 1899.

Connecticut State Register and Manuals, Hartford, CT: Secretary of State, 1954, 1970, 1974.

Cooke, Edward S., Jr., *Fiddlebacks and Crookedbacks: Elijah Booth and Other Joiners in Newtown and Woodbury, 1750-1820*, Waterbury, CT: Mattatuck Historical Society, 1982.

Cothren, William, *History of Ancient Woodbury*, 3 vols., Waterbury, CT: Bronson Brothers, 1854-79 and W.R. Seeley, 1871-79.

Cronin, William, *Changes in the Land: Indians, Colonists, and the Ecology of New England*, New York: Hill & Wang, 1983.

Crofut, Florence S. Marcy, *Guide to the History and Historic Sites of Connecticut*, New Haven, CT: Yale University Press, 1937.

Dannenburg, Elsie Nicholas, *The Story of Bridgeport*, The Bridgeport Centennial, Inc., Bridgeport, CT: The Brewer-Borg Corp., 1936.

Davis, Burke, *Yorktown*, New York: Rinehart, 1952.

deForest, John William, *History of the Indians of Connecticut*, Hamden, CT: The Shoe String Press, 1964.

Deming, Dorothy, *Settlement of Connecticut Towns*, (Published for Tercentenary Commission), New Haven, CT: Yale University Press, 1933.

Education Study Committee, *Know Your Schools*, Newtown, CT: League of Women Voters of Newtown, Inc., 1983.

Fitzpatrick, John C., *The Diaries of George Washington*, New York and Boston: Houghton Mifflin Co., 1925.

Forbes, Allan and Cadman, Paul F., *France and New England 1925-29*, Boston: State Street Trust Co., 1925.

Gardner, Robert, *Anglicans to Americans: Trinity Episcopal Church, Newtown, Connecticut*, New York: Walker & Co., 1982.

Geller, Hubert F., "Connecticut Played Major Role in Winning of the Revolution," (Section F, 1-3), Bridgeport, CT: *Bridgeport Sunday Post*, July 6, 1975.

George, James Hardin; Smith, Allison Parish; Johnson, Ezra Levan, *Newtown's Bicentennial 1705-1905*, New Haven, CT: Tuttle, Morehouse and Taylor, 1906.

Hallock, Julia Sherman, *Broken Notes from a Gray Nunnery*, Boston: Lee & Shepard Publishing Co., 1896.

Hawley School, *Chronological List of Events: 1922-1972*.

Hurd, D. Hamilton, *History of Fairfield County*, Philadelphia: J.W. Lewis and Co., 1881.

Johnson, Jane Eliza, Comp., *Newtown's History and Historian, Ezra Levan Johnson*, Newtown, CT: 1917.

Kates, Brian, "Six Continuing Armyological Digs in Redding," (Section FL 1-2), New York: *New York Sunday News*, August 17, 1975.

League of Women Voters of Newtown, *Profile of Public Education in Newtown*, Newtown, CT: April, 1970.

Lucas, Mary R., Ed., *Newtown Congregational Church 250th Anniversary Year 1714-1964*, New Haven, CT: Newtown Congregational Church, 1964.

Mahan, A.T., *The Influence of Sea Power Upon History, 1660-1783*, Boston: Little, Brown and Co., 1889, (1940 edition).

Newtown Academician, Pupils of Newtown Academy, Newtown, CT: July, 1853.

Newtown Bee, The, Newtown, CT: Bee Publishing Co., issues throughout 20th century.

Newtown, Connecticut: Past and Present, (two editions), League of Women Voters of Newtown, New Haven, CT: 1955, 1975.

Newtown Historical Society, *Bicentennial Tapes of Newtown Citizens*, 1976.

Newtown Parks and Recreation Commission Minutes, 1955-1970.

Newtown, Town of, *Annual Reports*.

"Newtown's 250th Anniversary," (Special supplement), Newtown, CT: *The Newtown Bee*, August 5, 1955.

Nichols, Peter, *Account Book of Peter Nichols, 1813-1814*.

Osborne, Norris Gilpin, *History of Connecticut*, 5 vols., New York: States History Co., 1925.

Pfeiffer, Marianne, "Indians of Southern New England," (a chart), Old Lyme, CT: 1985.

Plan of Development, Newtown, Connecticut, New Haven, CT: Technical Planning Associates, 1969.

Quarrier, Sid, "The Geology of Newtown," (unpublished report), Hartford, CT: Natural Resources Data Center, Department of Environmental Protection, July 8, 1975.

Rice, Howard C., Jr. and Brown, Ann S. K., *The American Campaigns of Rochambeau's Armies 1780-1783*, New Jersey: Princeton University Press, 1972.

Roberts, Kenneth Lewis, *Oliver Wiswell*, New York: Doubleday, Doran and Co., 1940.

Rockwell, George L., *The History of Ridgefield, Connecticut*, Ridgefield, CT: George L. Rockwell, 1927.

Schmidle, Mae S., *Newtown, Ye History*, Newtown, CT: 1979.

Scott, Robert B., "Bedrock Geology of Southbury Quadrangle," (Report #30), Hartford, CT: Connecticut Department of Environmental Protection, 1974.

Scudder, Susan J., *The Story of Two Centuries of the Congregational Church, Newtown, Connecticut 1714-1914*, NewHaven, CT: Tuttle, Morehouse and Taylor, 1914.

Sellers, Helen Earle, *Connecticut Town Origins: Their Names, Boundaries, Early Histories and First-Families*, Stonington, CT: Pequot Press.

Shelton, Jane deForest, *Salt Box House*, New York: The Baker and Taylor Co., 1914.

Shepard, Charles Upham, M.D., *Geological Survey of Connecticut*, New Haven, CT: B.L. Hamlen, 1837.

Smith, Mortimer, *One Hundred Years of Schools in Newtown*, Newtown, CT: Bee Publishing Co., 1946.

Snow, Dean R., *The Archaeology of New England*, New York: Academic Press, 1980.

Spiess, Mathias, *The Indians of Connecticut*, New Haven, CT: Yale University Press, 1933.

Storrs, Edwin, "To the Twentieth Century," (Special Supplement, Newtown's Industries, Past and Present), *The Newtown Bee*, Newtown, CT: Bee Publishing Co., September 1, 1972.

Tiemann, H.N., Secretary, *Minutes of the Men's Literary and Social Club of Newtown Street, 1912-1920*.

Todd, Charles Burr, *In Olde Connecticut*, New York: The Grafton Press, 1906.

Trinity Parish, *Consecration of the Fourth Church Edifice, Newtown, Connecticut 1882*, Newtown, CT: 1882.

Trumbull, Benjamin, *A Complete History of Connecticut*, 2 vols., New London, CT: H.D. Utley, 1898.

Whipple, Chandler, *The Indians in Connecticut*, Stockbridge, MA: Berkshire Traveler Press, 1972.

Whitridge, Arnold, *Rochambeau: America's Neglected Founding Father*, New York: The Macmillan Co., 1965.

Wilcoxson, William Howard, *History of Stratford, Connecticut 1639-1939*, Stratford, CT: The Stratford Tercentenary Commission, 1939.

Wilson, Lynn, *History of Fairfield County*, 3 vols., Chicago and Hartford: S.J. Clarke Publishing Co., 1929.

Ye Olde Berkshire Hills, (Prepared for the Housatonic Railroad), New York: Press of American Bank Note Co., 1891.

MAPS

Beers, D.G., *Bicentennial Map of the Town of Newtown, Connecticut*, Newtown, CT: Bicentennial Committee, 1905.

Bridgeport and Newtown Turnpike Company, (original map), 1801.

Colles, Christopher, *Survey of the Roads of the United States of America*, (plates of road from Stratford to Poughkeepsie), 1789.

Connecticut State Highway Department, *Plan for Construction of the Bridgeport Road in the Town of Newtown*, October 29, 1927.

Fagan, L., *Map of Town of Newtown*, Philadelphia: Richard Clark, 1854.

Kellogg, F.J., Engineer, *Town of Newtown 96-33*, (13 sheets), Hartford, CT: Connecticut Department of Transportation, Dec. 18, 1908.

Newquist, Ruth, Newtown *Bicentennial Map — The American Revolution 1776-1781*, Newtown, CT: The League of Women Voters of Newtown, Inc., September, 1975.

Index

Know all men by these presents that wee o[f]
to potatuck in the Colloney of Connecticut for
Coats. four blankets four buffalis Coats four
of lead ten Hatchets ten pound of powder fforty [Knives]
have done settle may more fully appear wt say we
Confirmed; and by these presents do fraly fully and ab[solutely]
unto William Geanes Justis Bryh and Samuel
A Certain tract of Land Cituate lying and being
as followeth. vist Bounied South upon pine Gu[?]
Southwest upon Fairfiel Bounds, northwest on th[e]
by milford men at or near Senotonoad and South E[?]
dunning two miles from the river Eight against
Eight miles and in bredth six miles be tt more [or less]
Comodities thereunto Belonging or in any roife [?]
Justice Bryh and Samuel Hawby Junr their
to their owne proper use benefit and behoo[f]
and nunnawduk for us oue heirs Executors
to and withe the sd William Ganes Justes Br[yh]